Small Business
Big Ideas

video

e-mail

social
media

LOCAL
INTERNET
MARKETING

pay-per
click

mobile

articles

Published by Offline Profits Publishing, LLC Houston, TX
ISBN: 978-0615543284

The Publisher has strived to be as accurate and complete as possible in the creation of this book.

This book is not intended for use as a source of legal, business, accounting or financial advice. All readers are advised to seek services of competent professionals in legal, business, accounting, and finance field.

In practical advice books, like anything else in life, there are no guarantees of income made. Readers are cautioned to rely on their own judgment about their individual circumstances to act accordingly.

While all attempts have been made to verify information provided in this publication, the Publisher assumes no responsibility for errors, omissions, or contrary interpretation of the subject matter herein. Any perceived slights of specific persons, peoples, or organizations are unintentional.

For more information, please visit www.offlineprofitspublishing.com

Small Business
Big Ideas

Table of Contents

CHAPTER 1

ONLINE PROFITS FROM THE OFFLINE WORLD

By Jack Mize

The internet is getting smaller.

It's true. Every day consumers are turning to the internet to find local products and services.

The shift in focus of internet searches from global general research and entertainment to local consumers going online, rather than opening that fat yellow book, has caused industry giants like Google and Yahoo to make swift changes in the way they return results to online surfers.

Just go to Google and type in the term *Weight Loss*. You are no longer bombarded with just page after page of e-books and online diet programs. Now you are presented with a map of Local weight loss providers, listings and phone numbers of fitness professionals, nutritionists and dieticians right in your own back yard.

We are still in the Wild West of online communication and there has never been a time when the playing field has been this level to allow local small businesses to engage in the same marketing game as huge corporations.

To be clear, I'm not talking about E-commerce, the selling of digital products, e-books, videos, online courses. I'm talking about local brick and mortar businesses that serve local customers.

That is the sweet spot of Local Internet Marketing. The selling of products and services that can be marketed online, but cannot necessarily be fulfilled online. Technology has had meteoric growth over the last 15 years. The things that we are able to do online evolves and increases daily. But the fact is, there are some services that can't be fulfilled online and must be provided locally, such as:

- Home Remodeling
- Lawn care
- Massage Therapy
- Pool Cleaning
- Medical Treatment

These are just a fraction of things that must be fulfilled offline, but can certainly be marketed online.

Then there are products and services that can be bought and fulfilled online but are still primarily thought of as local, brick and mortar purchases. For example:

- Real Estate
- Furniture and Appliances
- Automobiles

These are items that are available online but have a strong emotional attachment to the purchase. Consumers want to feel them, smell them and touch them in order to make a buying decision.

Before we start talking about the tactical side of Local Internet Marketing we need to get inside the mind of the local consumer. This shouldn't be hard because we all, at some point, maybe weekly, perhaps daily, are local consumers. So we shouldn't have to make a wild guess about their behavior.

Let's use flat screen televisions as an example. If you haven't already purchased one, you probably will the next time you are in the market for a new TV.

Time to be honest. If you purchased a flat screen in the last year, you probably researched it online, looked at reviews online, priced it online, and narrowed your choice of brands and models based on your findings... online. The one thing you probably didn't do online was push the "BUY NOW" button.

Chances are, you got in your car and drove 20 minutes to the local electronics store and paid more than you would have online! Why? Because we live in a "microwave" society. WE WANT IT NOW! And that's ok. I do the same thing. If you didn't, you are the exception and I commend you.

The internet is now the number one source for finding local business information. Local consumers are going online to research products and services and then making their purchases offline from local businesses.

If you own a local business, consumers are looking for you.... Right Now! On the internet. Are you there?

A few years ago it was actually debatable. Local small

businesses could ask themselves "Do I really need a website? Is this internet advertising really worth the investment"?

Well the debate is over folks. Local small businesses desperately need to be found online. The problem is most also have no idea how to be found online. Those that do manage to be found are often times delivering the wrong message.

You see, there really two things you have to get right to have a successful internet marketing campaign: Traffic PLUS a compelling message and/or offer. You get this simple formula down and good things will happen. You get only one of them right and nothing happens.

Traffic + Compelling Message = More Customers

Before we begin, let me go ahead and knock down a couple of obstacles you might have.

"But Jack, marketing online is beyond my reach. Online advertising is not something I can afford right now."

OK. What if I told you that you can effectively start your Local Internet Marketing Campaign with a budget of nothing, zero, nada.

You can certainly benefit from the services of an experienced Internet Marketing provider and the cost will probably pay for itself in a very short time. But if you don't have a budget at all, don't stop reading, you are still in the game.

The principles and strategies I'm talking about can be implemented with no money invested. If you have a little time to invest, you can make this happen very quickly.

This isn't about Pay Per Click, buying advertising, hiring SEO Gurus. What I'm going to share with you is definitely within your reach.

"But Jack, I don't know anything about computers or building websites."

Good. Then you are not far behind me. This is a "NO TECHIE" zone. Everything I talk about can be put into play by you are your staff. If you can write an email or type a Word document then you can start a Local Internet

Marketing campaign.

Let me be crystal clear on this one point:

Local Internet Marketing
IS NOT ABOUT HAVING A WEBSITE!

What? "But Jack, I thought that's what internet marketing was." Not when we are focusing on local consumers. That's right. Local Internet Marketing is about getting your **compelling message and information** in front of local consumers and that's not necessarily a website.

A local search study* revealed that a website was actually fourth on the list of what consumers expected to find when searching for local businesses online.

What beat it out?

1. Phone Number - Local Consumers want to contact you. They are ready to engage.
2. Address - Where are you? Are you close enough for me to do business with?
3. Hours of operation - When can I do business with you?

4. Website - Only then are local consumers ready to check out a website, if available.

What does this mean? Local consumers are ready to buy. They are ready to engage. Often times they've done their legwork and have made a decision.

Recent market research revealed that 92% of all local searches will eventually convert into a sale**. Your compelling message needs to let them know that you can fulfill that sale. And that doesn't have to be a website.

Local Internet Marketing Is Getting Your Compelling Message Findable In Multiple Places When Local Consumers Are Looking For Your Product or Service!

Get it? Got it? Good. Let's get this party started. On Your Mark.....

What Is My Compelling Message?

Before you even think about turning on your computer you have to know the answer to this critical question. "Should I market what I do, or who I am?"

This is a challenging question indeed. Marketing "what you do" refers to advertising and promoting your services. In other words, if you're a plumber, you would advertise your ability to fix leaks, install water heaters or assist in remodeling.

Marketing "who you are" is about establishing your brand in the market. As a plumber, marketing who you are would mean establishing yourself as "Zippy, the reliable, high quality solution to plumbing problems". It would mean emphasizing the qualities that set you apart from your competition, whatever those may be.

This may be easier to answer than you think, but you must check your ego at the door. Are local consumers searching for "24 hour emergency plumber" or "Zippy, the reliable plumber"?

Do you need more customers today or do you need to start building a brand? There is nothing wrong with either answer, depending on your situation. For purposes of this discussion I'm going to assume you are in the "I need more customers now" category.

Marketing who you re is how you build your brand and that

can be a slow process. Unless you have the steady business and advertising budget to mix it up with Nike shoes, Sam Adams beer or Calvin Klein polo shirts my suggestion is market "What You Do" until you build that comfort zone. As your budget allows, you can gradually invest in brand building at the same time.

Marketing "what you do" is the best way to convert leads into immediate business. When a customer has a flooded basement due to a broken pipe, they're not looking for great story telling and brand identity—they are looking for somebody who can fix their problem immediately.

Speak to problems and provide solutions.

Each of your prospects has a problem. As a landscaper, your prospects need their trees trimmed or their grass cut. As a travel agent your prospects need someone to put together a vacation within their budget. Don't beat around the bush. Your message should not bore them with statistics or long stories. If you run an air conditioning service, don't spend time advertising how many trucks you own or how highly qualified your technicians are. Instead, tell your prospects that you'll get their A/C working again immediately. When your prospects are looking for your services, they don't want to be informed or entertained. They want a solution to a problem.

Here's an exercise. Get out a pad and paper and answer these questions.

If someone were to ask "What do you do?" What would your answer be? Remember get your ego out of the way. You want customers.

Would you answer "I'm an independent Liquid Pressure Valve Engineer" or "I fix broken pipes fast and affordably." Which one would get you more customers? So a compelling message would be "My Town Emergency Plumber - On Call 24 Hours." It's not that hard.

How do potential customers look for your product or service?

Think about how you would look for a real estate agent. Would you look for "My City real estate agent?" Probably not. That message doesn't speak to a problem or provide a solution.

Instead, depending on your needs, you might search for

"My city first time home buyer help" or "my city rent to own condos". This is how local consumers that are ready to buy search online. If you are a real estate agent with knowledge in these markets then YOU being the solution to these problems is what will make up your compelling message.

Equally important is closing your message with a strong call to action. Once you've told your audience that you can solve their problem give them jolt to pick up the phone and call!

"First Time Home Buyers.

Confused by the buying process? I can help.

Together we can find your perfect

My Town Dream Home.

Stop putting it off—call today!"

555-555-5555

Write down 10 compelling messages for your business. Pick the best three and then make them findable online.
You have your top three? Good. Now how do you make them findable without having or programming a website?

Glad you asked. Remember "No Techie Zone". Local Internet Marketing = Being Findable in multiple places when local consumers are looking for your products or services. We are going to do this by opening what I call "Lead Valves."

What are Lead Valves? Independent, compelling messages driving consumers to your offer.

Step 1. Have all your business info on hand. You want to make sure it is consistent in your compelling messages. Don't make consumers work to find your contact info.

Step 2. Have an email address and password picked out that you can use when setting up your online listings.

Step 3. Start opening the Lead Valves

Google Places - Google gives you the opportunity to tell local consumers about our business and it's free. www.google.com/local/add/

Merchantcircle.com - Free business listing and directory for you to add your compelling message.

Online Classifieds - Craigslist.org, Backpage.com, OLX.com are just a few online classified sites that you can put your compelling message absolutely free. Make sure your headlines incorporate "what you do" and not "who you are." Many businesses make the mistake of putting "Acme Mortgage" as the listing headline rather than "My Town Low Down Payment Home Loans."

InfoUSA.com - This directory feeds hundreds of other business directories so your information and message can spread quickly.

Get started with these Lead Valves today. It certainly isn't an exhaustive list. Do some research of your own and see what free directories and classifieds show up when you do a search for local products and services. Then add your business with a compelling message and strong call to action.

If you follow these steps and make sure your message speaks to problems and provides solutions, then don't be surprised when new customers start saying "I found you on the internet!"

*TMPDM/ comScore
**comScore, Hitwise, Technorati and RealTimeStatistics.org

ABOUT JACK

Jack Mize is a Local Internet Marketing expert and small business consultant who helps businesses get more customers by making them findable when local consumers are looking for their products and services.

Jack's focus on the difference in online searching behavior of consumers when they are looking to buy locally led him to develop his method of opening "Lead Valves". This strategy allows local businesses to be found in multiple places instead of focusing on just a web site.

By identifying problems that local consumers need to solve locally and creating "Lead Valves" that provide the solution, Jack has developed a system that is laser focused on the quality of the conversion rather than the quantity of internet traffic.

One of the biggest features of this method is that the "Lead Valve" sources have nothing to do with paid traffic like pay per click or online banner ads.

In 2009 Jack began teaching his Lead Valve strategy to Local Internet Marketing consultants and small business owners around the world. He has been credited with saving businesses and changing lives.

To learn more about Jack Mize and receive up to date information on what's working in Local Internet Marketing by one of the leading experts, visit www.JackMize.com

CHAPTER 2
THE POWER OF FOCUS

By Doug Simpson

Advertising is critical to the success of local businesses. If you own or operate one, you have been approached by many sales people offering the golden key to success. But all too often that key fits the salesman's commission account and not your business's front door.

I spent decades in managing my own and others' businesses before working for a regional newspaper. Several things became apparent to me over those years.

The first thing is that business owners are not always good marketers. Business owners and managers are involved in operating their business, managing the staff, controlling expenses, developing their service, maintaining a viable inventory, servicing customers, and all the other many facets of operating a business. As a business owner, you are an expert at what you do. You may have chosen your profession, inherited it, or simply fell into somehow by default.

I have managed a number of businesses for myself and others. Some I chose and some chose me. But to survive in them, I had to become an expert at that particular part of the business world.

One business that chose me was a commercial sign shop. I created a hand carved wooden sign for a friend which somehow pulled me into starting a business I knew nothing about. My first few hand painted signs were only paid for because either the client didn't know how bad the sign was or he was just too polite to refuse to pay for it.

One of my competitors with a fantastic outlook on life gave me lessons on how to professionally paint signs. I was trained by an expert and I became an expert sign painter. My signs appeared throughout the area and some are still there some twenty years later.

In the sign business, it always amazed me how a person would spend all their assets, time, and energy to open a new business. They might plan for years how to finance it, design the floor plan, study to learn what they needed to know to operate it, find a location, and set up the business.

Then once they were ready to open they would call me to come and put up a sign for them. I would quote a price and time to produce and mount the sign. The response would often be, "Oh that is too much money. I spent my entire budget on the store." Not only was the sign not in the budget, but marketing of any kind had not been included in their budget.

Most business owners are not marketers and most advertising sales people are not experts at your business or any other kind of business. Some advertising representatives are experts at producing advertising, but few or none are experts at marketing your particular local business.

Because of this, advertising often fails to generate the expected return on money spent.

The second thing that became apparent to me is that businesses fail to market their expertise.

My goal with a sign was to design something that would generate as much traffic as possible for that business by getting people's attention and delivering a quick concise message about the focus of the store.

Businesses that consider themselves to be local do so because of focus. Your focus may be by geographic reach, product lines, types of service, or field of interest. Or maybe you are local because you own your business. But your business has or was originally created with a focus.

Look around your city as you drive and observe business signs. You will discover that a large part of them tell you little or nothing about what the business is about. And even more amazing is that some of them are not even legible as you drive by.

In talking with clients about signs and newspaper advertising they often want to put a book of information on a four foot sign or a 2 column by 3 inch newspaper ad. They want to make sure the reader knows everything they have to offer. Some want to use their favorite odd script or a poorly designed logo and in the process, the sign is not legible and no one reads the ad. Successful billboards have five words or less. They are focused on a single concise message.

Focus on the top 20% of your sales whether it is a product or service. The top 20% will more than likely comprise 80% of your total sales. And if that is the case, it will also appeal to 80% of the people you want to reach. The other 80% of your products and services only appeal to about 20% of the people. Wouldn't you much rather attract 80% of the people instead of 20%?

For great results, find the top 5% of your sales. Devote 80% of what you do advertise to this 5% and the other 20% to the remaining 15% of the top 20%.

Confusing? Let me put it this way – it is important that you focus the bulk of your advertising on the bulk of your sales. It is much easier to multiply sales on something that is already selling and people are actively seeking than to create sales on something that has little demand.

The third thing that I find is that businesses advertise their name and not what they do or need they fulfill. In the advertising world this is often called branding or name awareness.

When people look for your business they have a need and they are looking to satisfy that need. That need may be in reaction to pain. In North Texas as I write this information we are 42 days into triple digit heat and expecting 30 more days. Right at the moment it is 109 degrees.

If my air conditioner quits working, I will be in pain and have a desperate need. I will immediately be looking for one of two things – either an emergency repair business that offers immediate freezing cold air with 24 hour service or a hotel room. Let me assure you it is near impossible to get a relaxing night's sleep in a 100 degree plus bedroom.

Focus on the customer that is already seeking your service rather than trying to convince a customer they need your service.

A couple of years ago we had a series of tornado generating weather days in our area. Tornado condition weather usually produces damaging hail even if the actual tornado doesn't fully develop or reach the ground. Our neighborhood was one of several that received severe hail damage.

Within 24 hours the streets seemed to be filled with roofing companies and temporary paintless dent removal shops. These businesses did not have to convince anyone that their service was needed to almost immediately book months of service work.

There are mini-disasters every day in your neighborhood.

Your products and services serve the need created by those situations, whether physical, emotional, or spiritual.

A successful marketing program will focus on those needs. One of most effective ways to focus in on these needs is the Internet. Using this tool allows you to speak directly to the customer right in your own neighborhood, city, or region.

The Internet is the king of focus. You can reach right into the desk top of customers within a few feet or hundreds of miles from your store front. You can even put a message directly into their hand or pocket with the touch of a button.

Type a single word into a search engine and you will instantly have a list of millions of sites with that single word as a part of the site. Type in multiple related words and the list gets a bit smaller. Change the words to a descriptive phrase in parenthesis and the list is reduced to very few and maybe even no results.

Search the Internet for the focus of your business and you will find other businesses, individuals, interest groups, and institutions connected with your business interests.

If you search through Google or Yahoo using the one word that best describes your business will it show up in the search results? Are you in the first page list of sites? If you are not in the first ten results, your message will probably not be seen. Are you on the Internet at all?

Remember, the key is focus!

Can you describe your business in one word? Can you name your top selling product line or service in one word? Can you sum up the benefit you provide to your community in one word? Maybe it takes two or three words, or even five words, but if it takes you 5 minutes to tell someone about your business you are missing focus.

Your customer, regardless of age or interest, is involved with what is termed new media in the advertising field. But the elements of new media are now the core of how people communicate, shop, research, and navigate the streets of our world.

The most dominate factor in this digital web of devices and applications is the ability to ask a question and get an immediate answer. People have become accustomed to quick answers and easily found information because of the

Internet, cell phones, and even pocket size computers.

As any experienced business owner knows, there is no golden key to quick success. It is a very complicated and sometimes very long process to develop a strong customer base, growing sales volume, and effective business plan. Because of that we sometimes get so complicated no one outside our business really understands what we do.

Discover the absolute simplest way you can describe your business. Focus in on the key elements of what your customer is looking for and how you provide that service. Once you have the focus and properly insert it into the magic of the Internet, it might just turn out to be a golden key!

ABOUT DOUG

Doug Simpson started his business career at the age of eleven selling doughnuts door to door after school. Two years later he was running a cash register and stocking shelves in the local super market. His chain store experience started at eighteen as an assistant manager. Doug's retail career finally spanned five major chain stores including managing a Wal-Mart store.

Owning his own business was always a dream that became a reality in the form of a commercial sign shop that included hand lettering windows to designing and erecting 20' highway signs. The sign shop was one of two businesses started and sold. What followed was a family owned corporation that created the number one online retail store in its niche in the United States.

Doug's first love is conquering the challenge to create and maximize successful endeavors. He has done this with retail and service business, writing books, and helping other people achieve personal and business goals. Serving ten years as the pastor of a Baptist church, Doug experienced the joy of helping people find the various aspects of prosperity.

After selling his successful corporation, Doug is concentrating on assisting people achieve personal success by using the tools that they already possess. Personal success brings a joy and mindset that permeates everyone around them and generates success in business and career.

Visit his website at www.doug-simpson.com or contact him at doug@doug-simpson.com.

CHAPTER 3

DISCOVER WHY ALL BUSINESS OWNERS NEED A FACEBOOK FAN PAGE

By Fabio Moro

The Internet started in 1969 as the ARPANET, which was a Defense Department system designed to let survivors of a nuclear attack to share files and information. From a handful of crudely connected top-secret computers, the Internet has grown to a previously unimagined scope of influence revolutionizing how people conduct their daily lives both personally and professionally. Today, using the Internet is commonplace. As a result, companies of all sizes are advertising and marketing on the Internet to spread their message and brand into the public consciousness.

In an effort to market online, many companies create a website and believe they are using the Internet to market. However, a website is useless unless someone finds the website. Until Social media came along the name of the online marketing game was to rank high in search engines such as Google and Bing. People who consulted in this burgeoning field typically adopted the title of SEO consultant. For a time, a good SEO consultant could help drive a considerable amount of leads to a business by using various strategies to ensure a surfer, typing a particular keyword or phrase, found a website. However, the Internet changes fast and SEO, while still important, is now only a piece to developing a strategic and comprehensive Internet marketing based strategy. Enter the world of social media.

What Is Wrong with Traditional Marketing?

Businesses owners intuitively understand that merely having a website is not enough regardless of how well designed the website might be both from an aesthetic and marketing point of view. Real estate professionals use a common expression. You will often hear people suggest that real estate is primarily about location. Well, Internet marketing is similar to real estate in that location, or positioning, matters. You need to position your brand in the right locations so that people will see your brand, relate to your brand, and take action.

Think of the internet as a highway. Imagine a potential

customer, or client, driving down the highway. As the driver proceeds down the highway, the driver takes in a multitude of stimuli that all compete for attention. Now ask yourself, how would you get that potential customer's attention and stand out?

Perhaps you would have a giant billboard. Perhaps you would create an attention grabbing radio advertisement. Perhaps you would use both a billboard and a radio advertisement. Regardless of what you do, that billboard ad needs traffic driving past it; otherwise, the billboard becomes useless, and the radio ad, without listeners, becomes useless.

Ponder for a minute your own Internet marketing efforts. Do you have a website no one sees? Do you have a social media account to which no one listens? Perhaps the time has come for considering ways to garner traffic via the search engines and social media--specifically Facebook.

Why Facebook

Facebook is a tremendous vehicle that generates responsive traffic. Facebook creates a dynamic and relationship oriented way to interact with potential customers and clients who share a common interest. Facebook has experienced unprecedented growth precisely because of the ability to create an online community of like-minded individuals. Instead of connecting computers together through the Internet, Facebook connects people through the Internet. In fact, Facebook has grown so rapidly the almighty Google recently created a competing social networking site called Google Plus. At the time of this writing, Google Plus is still in beta testing. Hence, I will be writing an update to this chapter once more is known about Google Plus as a marketing opportunity.

The Power of Facebook

Facebook is an absolute powerhouse in terms of building an online community of potential prospects. Because of unique features within Facebook, business owners can target prospects with a precision similar to radio or television, but I would argue, even more targeted.

Currently, Facebook has well over 700 million active users. Consider the previous statement for a moment. Seven hundred million users is nearly double the population of the United States of America. This means even a small-business owner in a small town will have people in their immediate community using Facebook in some capacity. Of these users, only a small fraction need respond to your marketing message to help generate more business leads.

Why you Need Fans and Trust

An effective Facebook presence, for a local business, requires building a customer base (fans) that reside in the local area. Building trust is a critical outcome of relationship building and socializing. Often, a business owner asks why socializing is necessary. Think of this process not so much as socializing, but as engaging in public relations and networking. Remember, Facebook, at the core, is a social networking site.

Marketing effectively via Facebook involves creating an online community built upon relationships, interaction, and trust. People generally are more open to buy from people they know, trust, and like. When a consumer knows the brand and trusts the brand, the consumer will be more apt to consume, or purchase, the brand.

All those ads on TV, and so forth, merely induce a person to think about the advertised product at the decision-making moment of purchase. Imagine an individual in a grocery aisle. The person is thirsty; he or she is at the soda isle, and the person sees an off-brand. Then, the person sees a name brand that he or she has come to know and trust. Assuming price is not an issue, which product will the person most-likely purchase? Most people, in the described scenario, will gravitate to the name brand product because of the trust factor.

Have you found yourself making a decision to purchase one product over another because you have at least heard of the brand? Social media provides an excellent way to build a niche community of followers who will come to know and trust your brand.

Running an effective social media campaign, whether on Facebook, Twitter, or anywhere else requires a time commitment, which some companies might view as an obstacle. However, social media consultants can help manage the process by sending out pre-approved offers and engaging your fan base. Moreover, basic interaction can be outsourced to a family member or idle coworker.

People spend a considerable amount of time on Facebook interacting and socializing. Many people will check their Facebook accounts several times a day. Some users even make Facebook their default homepage. The socializing aspect of Facebook makes it qualitatively different from Google or any other search engine.

Typically, people using Google are searching for something specific via a specific keyword or phrase. However, Facebook users primarily intend to interact and keep up with friends and family. This interactive quality is an important psychological factor to consider when developing a marketing strategy. An effective social media marketing strategy needs to be relationship-oriented and designed to build trust. An in-your-face car salesperson approach will fail. Instead, build a relationship and include non-intrusive marketing people will appreciate, such as a coupon offer (coupons are fantastic), or an announcement on a special, that people will consider useful.

Pay attention to fan feedback about your brand or product. The feedback provides useful information that can improve your business. Large companies spend a considerable sum to obtain customer feedback. Facebook has automatic customer feedback loops built in through interaction. The question feature, for example, can generate useful targeted information. Not all the feedback will be positive, but negative feedback provides an opportunity to respond, or make adjustments, to what might be real problems or concerns affecting business.

Paid and Free Facebook advertising

Similar to Google, Facebook has two fundamental ways of increasing exposure to a business. Either pay for advertising with Facebook ads or grow organically with free methods.

The Power of Like

One of the most important free methods for any business involves creating a Facebook fan page. Facebook fan pages, or Facebook Pages, allow anyone who finds your page to *like* the page. This Facebook *like* feature is incredibly potent and viral. What does viral mean? Well, in this case, think of viral as synonymous with word-of-mouth advertising on steroids.

Notice all the businesses creating incentives to *like* their page. Recently, more and more signs at checkouts and windows are appearing asking people to like their page. Fortune 500 companies are placing their Facebook fan page domain on business cards, flyers, and any other traditional advertising collateral.

The reason for marketing a fan page is that every individual who *likes* the fan page immediately becomes a prospect and immediately a member of an online community. By liking the page, the individual automatically enters into the fan page owner's personal database. In other words, the process creates Facebook's version of a mailing list.

Once the individual enters the community, any posts made to your Facebook wall will appear on their (the person who hit like) personal newsfeed. Yes, your post becomes *news*. Any individual looking at his or her newsfeed will see your post. The original post now has the potential of going viral through friends of friends.

Of course, the trick, as alluded to previously, is to post in a social fashion and engage fans in interesting and creative ways. This social point is worth repeating because this point is crucial to effectively networking the brand. People on Facebook exist to socialize and not to buy. Facebook users are not necessarily looking for a product, service, or information, and few people relish a barrage of advertising messages.

Quality content that is relevant, personalized, interactive, integrated, and authentic is vital to Facebook success. Fortunately, solid strategies and tactics exist to help disseminate an effective marketing message that meets all the aforementioned criteria. One of the best tactics involves bribery.

The Bribe Offer Strategy

The bribe strategy involves creating an engaging professional fan page with an incentive offer to press the like button. This classic bribe tactic borrows from list-building techniques used on traditional websites. The bribe, also referred to as the free giveaway, is extremely effective. In essence, the offer bribes the individual to press the like button in exchange for a valuable giveaway.

Look at this Fan page for an example
http://www.facebook.com/myfanpagebiz

The offer can be a valuable report, a coupon, or anything else that potential prospects would appreciate. Most businesses can easily create a coupon offering a nice discount for a product or service. Coupons provide an actionable incentive to visit your physical location. The key to successfully offering a coupon is to provide real discounts that will incentive the prospect to take action.

For example, if you own a car dealership, offering a coupon for a free cup of coffee will not incentivize people to take action and visit the dealership. However, if the offer is a coupon for $500 off the negotiated price, then people will come to your dealership. By the way, once the prospect is in the buying mood, you can always offer up-sells to recoup the $500, but you probably already knew that ☺.

The coupon giveaway also encourages people to notify friends who might be interested. Again, consider the dealership analogy. Perhaps the person who discovers your fan page does not need a car; however, the person might know someone who is in the market for a new car and would appreciate a nice discount. This is viral marketing online.

The Facebook Like Culture

Most Facebook users do not mind pressing the like button. Pressing like has become commonplace and few people view pressing like the same as giving away an e-mail address. The Facebook like culture is an important psychological factor in your Facebook marketing strategy. Some people will press like without critically thinking about what they liked or with any level of reflection. One reason for this is Facebook has a feature allowing users to hide posts in their individualized newsfeed. This hide feature creates a subconscious level of trust because people are psychologically reassured they can receive their coupon and avoid unwanted posts. At this point, you are probably asking yourself, "Well, what good will it do if people simply hide my posts in their newsfeed?" I will address the question now.

How to be a Facebook Socialite

Remember that people are on Facebook to socialize and not to buy. What this means is that posts need to be interesting, engaging, and fun so fans will not perceive the posts as blatant advertising. The idea is to engage your audience in a way that respects privacy and operates within the social norms and culture of Facebook.

Through dialogue and engagement, a certain percentage of people will like your post and even comment on your post. Moreover, some might even pass along the post by sharing it with their own friends and fans. This helps increase the viral aspect of your fan page—word of mouth.

As people discover and visit your fan page they will see information about your product or service that will induce people to call, do more research, or take action. (TIP: If you want to take your fan page to the next level, you can actually build an entire website inside of your fan page.) A percentage of visitors who are not already fans will *like* your page and receive the giveaway offer. Hence, the cycle repeats.

Ultimately, the goal is not to get fans; the goal is to get people to come to your store and use the coupon to buy something. Hence, I will repeat; the offer needs to be something that will incentivize the person to take action. The building of fans is just part of the process and not the end game.

This does not mean that you cannot have the occasional marketing related post. However, try to make the post a casual kind of marketing and not an in-your-face sales pitch. For example, you might want to create a quiz, or survey, asking people for their opinion on a new product coming out or their opinion on a related topic. You might run a contest. You can thank a person who recently visited your store or used your service. You could announce a customer of the week. Anything that helps engage and interact with your prospects is something you should consider.

Build Fans and Sales with Paid Ads

Okay, do you not like the casual social approach? Fear not, Facebook provides a way to market to your fans in a more direct manner. You can use Facebook ads. Facebook allows you to target ads by demographics. You can use Facebook to advertise only to your fans if you wish. Your fans will see the ad, but not consider the ad blatant because the ad does not appear in their newsfeed.

However, you can take your paid advertising a step further. You can market to Facebook users who are not already fans, but have demographics, or interests, that would be suitable targets. Facebook has incredible targeting power. You can target people by age, by interests, by level of education, by specific schools, by what they have already liked, by specific zip codes, and more.

You should know that you do not need a Facebook fan page to use the advertising feature; however, it is wise to have a fan page because having a fan page for the specific product or service you are marketing helps lower the cost of advertising. Facebook does not appreciate when people leave their system and redirected to another site. Having your ad link to a Facebook fan page instead of an outside website keeps the user inside Facebook, which Facebook likes—pardon the pun.

Are you starting to get the picture? Someone sees the ad, the person clicks the ad, the person sees your nice professional Facebook fan page, the person clicks like and receives a coupon, and the viral process begins again as a continuous database of potential targeted customers is built. Very powerful indeed! In fact, I am hard-pressed to think of a more powerful advertising medium at this time.

The purpose of this brief chapter has been to provide a broad overview of how to use Facebook Fan Pages to get your business in front of more eyes. Facebook is not a cure-all to all your internet-marketing needs. However, Facebook should be a piece of your overall marketing and advertising plan. In the future, I will be releasing information on how to further increase the effectiveness of your Facebook marketing by using Facebook applications to super-charge the viral aspects of Facebook.

ABOUT FABIO

Dr. Moro has been consulting and coaching in the field of Internet marketing for over a decade. He first became interested in Internet marketing while pursuing a master's degree in educational technology, in the department of educational psychology, at Texas A&M University and operated under the DBA Accent Consulting Group.

After graduation, Dr. Moro began to apply his knowledge to online marketing and began to master the art and science of SEO, PPC, Social Media, and Mobile Marketing to increase business leads and profitability. Today, Dr. Moro is known affectionately as the SEO Aggie and runs www.seoaggie.com.

In addition, Dr. Moro is Senior Leadership Advisor and Senior Partner with Corpus Optima. In this capacity, he is responsible for the design and implementation of Corpus Optima's leadership development products and services.

Dr. Moro is also an adjunct professor at the University of Phoenix, Concordia University, and Ashford University where he teaches graduate level courses in Leadership,

Human Resources Management, Organizational Theory and Practice, Public Speaking, Change Management, Ethics in Teaching, and Instructional design.

You can contact Dr. Moro through his Facebook fan page at www.facebook.com/myinternetmarketing

CHAPTER 4

USING YOUTUBE TO MARKET YOUR LOCAL BUSINESS

By Mike Taylor

Is video marketing something that is right for your business? Well, if you are in business to make money, the answer is probably, "Yes."

Video marketing is what the TV and Infomercial business is all about. Video is a multi-billion dollar industry – it is not a hobby. People consume videos and at an unbelievable rate and the networks know it. The networks produce video content to get you to watch paid commercials, and you do it. The commercials are expensive to run, but they work – that's why advertisers keep running them.

Simply put - video sells more than anything. Period.

Ours is a media-driven, MTV culture. We've been

conditioned to watch short, punchy videos. Our news is even delivered in short, 30-second sound bites.

'Short' is the important word here. Studying viewer attention show a drop off at 3 minute, and a second drop occurs between 4 and 5 minute. The maximum video length is around 7 minutes – about the length of time between TV commercials. After that, people are bored and have moved on to the next video.

Short videos that have a story engage your audience and let you speak directly to them. Compelling videos show how a product solves a problem, makes life good again, and end with a call for the viewer to take action – like Call Now! We want that all to action to happen before they leave. People obey compelling videos, too – especially when they stick around to hear the call to action...

Video production used to demand studios, expensive equipment and software. Making a video was simply out of the question unless you were a national chain. But that has all changed in the digital world.

Today, you can make your own compelling digital videos right on your computer desktop. You probably already have the software you need, too. You don't need expensive cameras or lights. In fact, many effective videos don't use a camera at all! And you don't need to appear onscreen, and you don't even need to speak.

In the next few pages you'll learn the secret of making your own short, 30-second to one minute long video that tells a story and helps you sell a product. Then you'll put it on your own YouTube channel, just like an expensive TV ad, but without the cost.

Why use You Tube?

You Tube is huge. People use YouTube a LOT. YouTubers watch over 1 Billion (with a 'B') videos per day. They upload 40 hours of video every minute.

I mean really huge. ComScore reported that Google properties (i.e., YouTube) serving <u>more than twice the videos served</u> by the next nine runners-up combined. But these are small operations: Fox Interactive, Yahoo, Viacom Digital, Microsoft, Turner Network, Disney Online and ESPN.

Also, viewers search for videos on interesting topics.

YouTube recently became the 2nd most searched site in the world, rivaling and surpassing Google searches.

If you are not tapping into this valuable stream of viewers, you are missing out. YouTube is free, and it's easy to use. You can put up as many videos as you want and share them with the world.

The video title and the words you use in the description and video tags are included in the YouTube index. When people search for a phrase, if your video's title, description or tags matches what they type in, they will find your video. You will get some of those one billion daily views.

Since YouTube is owned by Google, your videos have a good chance of showing in Google searches. YouTube videos can outrank Google's own map listings, and sometimes are second only to a paid listing.

A video search result displays a thumbnail image on a page full of text results. Your videos will draw a lot of attention because of the added impact of the stand-out picture.

YouTube also encourages people to share your videos. This makes it possible for your viewers to post your video on their Facebook wall or e-mail them to friends. YouTube lets you 'embed' your videos, which means you can put the video on your own web page.

Your next customers are on YouTube searching for videos, possibly about your service or product. Let's go help them find your solution to their problem.

Creating Your First Video

A good compelling video starts with a script. What do you want to say? Put each point you want to mention on its own line – it makes it easier to edit. Think in terms of the benefits a feature gives the customer, not the feature itself.

We already know videos must be short, and for a video under a minute, the script can be a few lines of text, definitely less than a page. You want bullet points, not chapters.

Your script should take the form of: Introduce a problem, show the results your solution provides, and ask them to buy or call you. That's pretty much it.

"Is your bathroom grout growing hair? Is it scaring your

children and neighbors? Zap-o-Grout will make grout cleaner then new, cleaner than you ever thought possible! Call Today, and stop scaring the kids!"

Easy stuff, right? I bet you can do better than that!

Now that we have a script, let's make some movies!

There are two types of videos to choose from – 'live action' (where you appear and speak) and 'slideshows' which use text and graphics to tell your story.

Option 1: A simple 'Live Action' video

Live action requires a video camera, but low-cost pocket cameras (like the Flip and Kodak Zi8) take great HD video. Even your digital pocket camera will take great movie clips. In a pinch, your computer's built-in camera will work fine.

If you choose live action, try to place yourself in front of your business or projects, or select a single color background. A plain background makes you more prominent on the screen.

A tripod is a cheap and effective way to get rid of camera-shake, greatly improving video quality. Your cameraman's job is simple: aim the camera, check your placement in the frame, and record. Go through your presentation, smile, speak clearly and remember to look at and speak to the camera. Turn the camera off and you have your video, ready to edit and post.

Option 2: A 'Slideshow' video

If you don't have a camera or don't want to be seen, you can make screen capture video of a prepared presentation.

Here's how to do that...

This easy way to make a desktop video uses PowerPoint (or KeyNote if you're on a Mac). Just create a slideshow, add the script we just wrote, one line or feature per slide, plus your call to action, and record it as a movie.

Start a new presentation and pick a theme for the slides. Add the titles, features and benefits from your script. Keep the show simple and use just one or two fonts and colors throughout the presentation. When you use bullet points, more than 3 per slide become hard to read. Make sure the last slide shows your contact information.

Include your logo, photos from your business or non-copyrighted art work to illustrate your slideshow. Transitions and text effects (used with restraint) add interest to your slides. When you are happy with slides and narration, save your work; it's time to record.

If you are on a Mac and using KeyNote, you are ready to record. Just go to you 'File' menu and click 'Record' and the slideshow starts. Step through your slideshow to record your video and narration. When you are happy with the results, select 'Export' to produce your video.

Capturing the screen to video on a PC does require screen capture software, but here are 2 free programs you can download to capture your slideshow and make your movies.

1. Jing (http://download.cnet.com/Jing/3000-13633_4-10744274.html) is a free, easy to use screen recording utility. It allows you to capture videos to disk or share them on-line. There is a 5 minute limit to the videos, but we already know that is more than enough time. Jing is also a handy screen capture utility that takes stills as well as video.

2. Camstudio (http://camstudio.org/) is another free recorder that produces sharp, crisp movies.

To record your video, start your slideshow, and launch the recorder. Place the capture region over the slide show, and hit 'record'. When the recorder counts down and starts recording, step through your presentation. Record your narration as you go. Click the 'stop' button to end the recording. Name your video, save it, and you are done.

If you want to edit your recordings, add titles, captions or background music, PC users have Movie Maker (it is on your machine). Mac users have iMovie, which is also pre-loaded on your Mac. These built-in editing programs let you put your business information and phone number on top of your live action videos.

Sharing Your Finished Video

All that's left now is to put your finished video on YouTube.

Log-in to YouTube and (you'll need to create an account if you don't have one). Just click 'Upload' to copy your video from your computer to YouTube. While it is uploading, edit your video's title and description.

Your title should include your service keywords and city name to help local customers find it. Start your description with your website's URL, including the 'http' part; this will let people click on your link to go to your website. Remember to include keywords describing your video in the 'title', 'description', and 'tags'.

Once the video has uploaded and it has been processed, it is ready for the world to see. Now you can promote your new video by sharing the link provided.

Your YouTube Channel

When you sign-up for YouTube, you get you own 'channel', or home page. You can add background images, logos, set the color scheme and generally personalize your channel. This is the place you'll put all your videos and where your viewers can interact with you. You also have control of what shows on your channel, including comments.

When you set up your channel, the channel name should be optimized, like your web site name, for maximum search value. Select either an image or logo for your picture and channel icon to help brand your channel. A completed profile will draw extra attention from locals, so include your home town and use descriptive keywords in your 'about me', 'location' and 'interests' sections.

The keywords you use in these areas determine where your video winds up in searches. Careful choice of words will results in better rankings and more views.

Promoting Your Video

YouTube searches favor popular videos – ones with lots of views, lot of shares, and lots of 'likes'. It is a 'Catch-22', but you video has to be popular in order for it to become popular. Don't be afraid to ask YouTube visitors to 'like' or share your video – the more it is shared, the easier it will be for others to find.

YouTube makes it easy to embed a video on your own web page. This is the perfect way to showcase your video on your own page. Imagine the impact it will have on your business - being able to spend 2 to 3 minutes explaining the value of your services to hundreds, or thousands, of people.

Make a video that explains each service you perform, put it on a page for that service, and let it introduce the service to viewers. The views it gets on your own page help make it more popular on YouTube as well.

You customize the embedded video size to fit best on your web page, and they give you code to paste into your web page. It's easy, and it's effective.

It's time you put your videos on the web, a billion viewers are waiting!

ABOUT MIKE

Mike Taylor is a local marketing specialist in southern California. Mr. Taylor brings 20 years of computer and IT experience to bear, helping local businesses get more clients. His computer experience ranges from COBOL and FORTRAN on mainframes to design and creation of modern object-oriented, database and internet programs.

This computer experience, along with most advanced tools available, allows Mr. Taylor to create high visibility, traffic, sales and leads generation for clients through multiple channels. His past and current client list includes DOD contractors, energy producers, newspaper publishers, commodity traders, manufacturers, entertainment and construction industries as well as numerous local retail businesses and non-profit organizations.

Mike has a special interest in applying advanced SEO research and principles to video, article and other forms of search marketing. For more information on these and other local marketing topics, visit
http://eAdvertiseMyBusiness.com
or contact mike@eAdvertiseMyBusiness.com

CHAPTER 5

USING VIDEO TO BUILD YOUR BUSINESS AUTOMATICALLY

By Virginia Drew

One of the continuing challenges to any business owner is building the business. To do this, you need to get new customers as well as sell more to existing customers. It is getting more and more difficult to get your message out to new prospects. When you call, you just get shoved off to their voice mail. No one returns phone calls. Fliers and brochures get tossed in the trash. Emails don't get read. 95% of new visitors to your website just leave without doing anything... never to return. Everyone gets so many sales calls that they are numbed by it all. How do you cut through the "noise" and get through to the prospect to get your message across?

These days, everyone loves to watch videos. Youtube.com gets 3 billion views per month. 24 hours of video are uploaded to youtube.com every minute. You can use this love affair with video to your advantage and convert more prospects to customers, sell more to existing customers, and get more referrals and testimonials to build your business 3 to 4 times faster with very little effort.

Types of Videos to Use

There are 3 types of videos that you will use for this strategy:

1. "Talking head" video: This video consists of you sitting in front of a camera and speaking to it. It is great for introducing yourself and establishing rapport with prospects, and will be used extensively for this purpose.

2. Slideshow video: Most people have been to a class or seminar where the leader put slides up on a screen which illustrated the points he was making. This type of video consists of the slides being shown one by one with you speaking in the background. It is used most often when you want to teach something to your audience, and will be used quite a bit for existing customers.

3. Screen capture video: This is used when you want to demonstrate something on the computer. You use software which records your computer screen as you go through the steps. It is very valuable for those who teach computer skills or have technology based services. For most businesses it is probably the one you will use the least.

What Videos Should You Create?

You should create videos any time you want to communicate. This includes videos for prospects, customers and visitors to your online properties (website, Facebook, Twitter, LinkedIn, etc.)

Most videos will be very short (one minute or less) except those that are meant to inform, which can be up to 10 or 15 minutes.

Prospecting Videos

Online prospecting:

The first thing you need to do is convince prospects to give you their contact information. Create a "bribe" to get visitors to sign up (opt in) to your list. This is your introductory offer. For example, an accountant may offer a free consultation and "audit assessment" wherein he reviews a prospect's last 3 years' returns to see how much additional refund they may be eligible for and let them know what "red flags" may be putting them at risk for an IRS audit. Whatever it is, it must have great value for the prospect.

Your first online prospecting video will send prospects to a squeeze page where they will be asked to give you their name and email address. It describes your introductory offer and links to the landing page on your website. Put the video on your Facebook, Twitter, or LinkedIn pages, or on your website. Place a link to the video in your email signature. Get this in as many places as possible to get many more prospects into your sales funnel.

Then, put a video on the landing page where you make your offer and ask prospects to give you their email address. It should spell out what the offer will do for the prospect. Maybe it helps them solve a problem or shows them how to improve their lives. People will not just give up their email anymore... there must be a good reason to do so.

Once you have their contact into, send them to a video that tells them what a great decision they made and describes the wonderful things they will be receiving. It should also make another offer to get them to call you immediately.

Once they are on your list, send a series of videos giving them great information. The easiest way to do this is to write down a list of FAQ. Answer each question in a short video (one minute or less). End each video with a call to action (i.e., call me with any questions).

80% of sales are made on the 5th to 12th contact, so if you don't continually follow up you will leave a lot of sales on the table.

Offline (Real World) prospecting:

Before he is ready to buy, the customer must know, like and trust you. At the time someone first calls to set up an appointment for a meeting you are virtual strangers. The wise use of video can help you develop some rapport and elevate you above the competition.

Immediately after you have set up a meeting, you should send the prospect an email with a video link. In the video, you speak directly to him. You are smiling and friendly and tell him what a pleasure it is to have spoken with him and how much you look forward to working with him. Direct him to your website to see samples of your work and testimonials from satisfied customers. If you don't have a website, ask him to call you for references. Reinforce the fact that you have set aside this time for him and to call you if he must cancel.

This video can easily double or triple your conversion rate, because the prospect will be impressed that you took the time to follow up with him and will start to think of you as an acquaintance. There will be a bit of rapport that develops. This will give you a huge advantage over anyone else that he will meet, because they are still strangers to him. It will also cut down on the number of "no shows".

The meeting you have will have one of 3 outcomes: They will buy from you, they will say "no", or they will "think about it". In any case, you should have a video ready to send. One will say how much you are looking forward to working with him. It will also reassure him that he made a great choice (you could again tell him how much experience you have and offer some testimonials). This will ease any "buyer's remorse". The second will let him know you are sorry it didn't work out, and leave the door open if they have any questions. The third will remind him why he should hire you. It should actually be a series of videos, so he thinks of you when he is ready to hire someone.

Other prospecting videos:

One way to get many referrals is to partner with a complementary business and cross refer your customers. Create a video that introduces yourself and invites possible strategic partners to contact you to discuss how you may help each other gain clients. This will save a lot of phone calls. This is much more effective than regular emails because the recipient will want to watch the video. It will also help start to build rapport.

Immediately after leaving a networking event, trade show, seminar or other event where you meet people and collect their business cards, you could send out a video. It would say hello, it was nice talking to you, and I would love to get together with you sometime. This reinforces you in the prospect's mind.

To get free PR, send an email with a video to the reporters who cover your industry, telling them why you are interesting, unique, or newsworthy. Or, try to piggyback onto current events. Timely submissions could get picked up by the media. You may get an interview in the newspaper or on TV. The addition of the video makes it easier to get through to an overworked reporter and makes it more likely that he will listen to you.

You may have prospects that have fallen off the radar because you didn't have a follow up system. Create a video that is friendly and inviting. Tell them you are thinking of them and if they have any questions or concerns to be sure to call you. It only takes a few minutes, and can generate a lot of new business from your "dead" list.

Customer Videos

Once a prospect becomes a customer, your focus shifts to giving him the best possible service and starting a long-term relationship. You also want to get referrals and testimonials. The following videos will assure that your customers are happy and that your business grows.

If your service takes an extended period of time with temporary disturbance, inconvenience or discomfort for your customer, send a video that explains what you will be doing. It shows him what to expect and reassures him that any disruption is temporary and an essential part of the job. It paints a picture of the expected outcome and emphasizes that the result will be well worth the temporary inconvenience or discomfort.

For example, a landscaper or pool installer may need to dig up large portions of the customer's yard and have heavy trucks traversing the lawn. A plastic surgeon's patients may need to endure temporary disfigurement or pain. A doctor who must treat a child over an extended period of time can use video to explain the procedure and reassure both the child and parent that it will soon be over.

When you provide a one-time service, follow up with a video to say thank you and let the customer know how much you enjoyed working with him. It will give you a professional image and leave a good impression. Ask for a referral or a testimonial and let him know you are available to answer his questions. Then, follow up with a video letting him know what other services you provide. He may want to do more business with you, now or in the future.

Create videos that contain information about each of your products. Embed these videos into email and drip feed new offers to current customers. This will allow you to cross sell or up sell without having to call them and without seeming to be pushy.

Send customers a video telling them how much you enjoy working with them and reminding them that the lifeblood of your business is new customers. They should be willing to give you a referral or testimonial. Using this video will relieve any awkwardness you may feel in asking for referrals and will get you a lot of new business. After you receive a video or testimonial, send them a "thank you" video.

If you are a professional or do any type of consultative selling, videos that keep the customer up to date on new developments in your field will be priceless for gaining customer loyalty. They also give you an excuse to contact your customers on a regular basis, thereby keeping your name at the top of their minds. This makes them less likely to look elsewhere when they need new services that you may be able to provide. One of the most common reasons for people changing professionals (accountants, etc.) is that they never hear from them, and therefore feel neglected. As Sy Sims (a New York discount clothing retailer) used to say: "an educated consumer is our best customer."

Use videos as content for your newsletter. No one reads email anymore. Newsletters that have long articles, though they may be of interest, are not read very much. Replacing those articles with videos will boost the number of people who actually consume the content.

Website Videos

There are several videos to put on your website to inform and entertain your visitors. People would rather watch videos than read, so using video will keep people on your site longer to learn about you and your services. You can replace any text that is currently on your site with a video. Better yet, include a video along with the text to accommodate those who want to read. This will also help attract the search engine spiders.

Put a "welcome" video on the homepage as an introduction to your company and the content of your site. It shouldn't be too long... as with most of the others it should only last a minute or so.

Include a video which introduces your customers to your "team." This gives a human face to people who normally would only be a voice on the phone or the sender of an email. People like to do business with people. Introducing your employees will massively increase customer loyalty. You should have an opt-in video, similar to the one on your squeeze page to encourage visitors to join your list.

You can also have "about us" and "contact us" videos.

Once You Have Made the Videos...What next?

Once you have created a video, how do you send it out? This is the easy part. Just go to www.youtube.com and create an account. Create a channel for your business and upload the video to the channel. If it is a content video -- one of the client education or FAQ videos -- you can make it public. The description should entice people to watch the video. Use words that a prospect would type in to find your services. Include the URL of your website at the beginning of the description so they can click through to your site. If appropriate, you can make it private so only the visitors who have the link will be able to see it.

Create the email in which you will send a link to the video. You will need an auto-responder. Start the email with the first name of the recipient and briefly introduce the subject of the video. Include a thumbnail image with a link to the video. Do not repeat what is in the video, because you want the recipient to want to watch it.

Begin with one or two videos. The prospecting follow up video is a good one to start with... it has been shown to triple or quadruple the conversion rate on first meetings with prospects. Next, do the FAQ videos and get them up on Youtube. They will attract new visitors to your website and therefore bring in new customers.

Add more videos until you have an entire set. You will think of others that fit your business. Let your auto-responder do the work. Do not send them out piecemeal. Establish a system and a routine and after a while it will run virtually on autopilot. You will be free to concentrate on giving the best possible service to your current customers.

ABOUT VIRGINIA

Virginia Drew began working online in 2008. She developed several online businesses, testing many methods of attracting traffic to the websites and converting that traffic to customers.

In 2010 she shifted her focus offline and, after speaking with several local business owners, realized they were not using the Internet effectively to get more customers. She then started researching ways that local business owners could focus the power of the internet to reach out to local consumers.

She soon learned that one of the most powerful "magnets" that local business owners could use is video. She now specializes in showing her clients how they can use video to convert more prospects to customers, to cross sell, and upsell current customers and increase the number of referrals they receive.

To contact Virginia, visit www.yoursalesdiva.com.

CHAPTER 6

FIVE KEY SECRETS TO WINNING WITH MOBILE MARKETING

By Blanche Hayden, PhD

Mobile marketing, a permission-based marketing tool, has been gaining popularity as a major channel for reaching customers and is quickly becoming THE key ingredient in creating a winning marketing formula. As a business owner, it's no longer an option to ignore mobile marketing if you want to stay engaged with your customers.

My name is Blanche Hayden and I am a local marketing expert who helps market small businesses to their local customer base, using the internet and mobile marketing. My life's path, from being an employee in diverse careers and being self-employed in many niches to now being a marketer, is the direct result of coming to the realization that without effective marketing, businesses will struggle to survive, much less grow and prosper. I became a marketing expert out of necessity and have turned it into a lifestyle.

I am fascinated and excited about mobile marketing and what it can do for the health and growth of small businesses. Join me as I share with you why I'm excited about mobile marketing and what key strategies you need to employ to use mobile marketing successfully.

The Emergence of Mobile Marketing

Let's go back in time (not so long ago) and examine the path to mobile marketing's emergence and resulting importance.

As people migrated to using the internet on their desktop computers, we found that eventually, traditional media by itself lost some of its glamour and attraction and thus, its effectiveness as a marketing method used to reach consumers. People couldn't wait to get home to get on their computers and do any number of activities on it, including playing games, communicating with others through emails and researching things.

People found they could research and learn about new items they wanted to buy or services they wanted to use.

Over time, they also realized they could use the internet to not only buy products online, but to find a business right in their hometown to buy those same items or to provide those services. Business owners (some slowly) began to realize that their businesses needed to have a web presence and that they needed to do some marketing on the internet. Thus internet marketing was born. One of the techniques business owners learned to use with internet marketing was email, to get their message to customers.

Of course, email was fabulous! Not only could customers "talk" with their friends and colleagues, but businesses could "talk" with them also. Email marketing took off like a banshee! I'm not sure what a banshee is, but you get the picture. The goal was for a customer to get your email message and voila! Now, a marketing funnel could be opened. Initially, the only problem was that everyone needed a computer for this avenue to be successful. Over time, of course, computer ownership became more widespread and yes, in a sense they even became mobile in the form of laptops. Heavy and cumbersome laptops, but they were mobile and effective, if you had a wi-fi connection.

We all know where this story goes. Email has become a

has-been. Over time, we all have become inundated with emails. Fewer than 20% of emails are opened these days and many messages don't even make it to your inbox, thanks to spam filters.

The other thing that's happening is that people seem to always be on the go, rather than at home. They're on the way to and from school or work, on the way to the store, on the way to meet friends, "on the way" to somewhere. As a result, they're not sitting at their PCs all the time.

The message I personally hear from small business owners these days is that the marketing methods they've been using for years aren't really working well for them anymore. They know they need to do something different. They just don't know what that "something" is.

Enter the mobile phone - a device that can fit into your pocket with ease. Yes, I know they were once as big and as heavy as bricks. Now, they're slim, lightweight, packed with features and loads of fun. And almost everyone has one.

Statistics show that over 90% of people in the United States now own and use a mobile phone. By the end of the 4th Quarter of 2011, the number of smartphones (super-duper, internet savvy and lots of fun mobile phones) in the United States is predicted to explode to about 50%. In fact, mobile phones already outnumber desktop computers at a ratio of 4 to 1.

The Importance of Mobile Phones

So what's the big deal with mobile phones and why is this exponential growth happening?

The mobile phone is always on, always with you and it's specific to one particular owner. Your mobile phone goes "on the way" with you. Wow! And marketing using mobile phones can provide an accurate measurement of your customers' engagement, since it's traceable to one specific person.

Mobile phones are fascinating. Tomi Ahonen, a bestselling author and expert in the mobile industry, has called the mobile phone the 7th Mass Media. A Mass Media is a media which is able to communicate to the greater masses. The original 6 mass media are: Print, Recording, Cinema, Radio, Television and the Internet.

What makes mobile phones the most unique of all the mass

media is that it is the only media that can do everything the other six mass media do as well. You can read using a smartphone, listen to music, watch movies, listen to the radio, watch TV shows and you can surf the web. Of course, you can also talk on the phone.

AND – mobile phones can send and receive text messages. What are text messages? Text messages, also known as SMS (Short Message Service), are akin to emails. A text message is a written communication sent between people using a mobile phone.

Let me get back to the "always on, always with you and specific to one particular owner" thing. This is critical to what's happening with mobile. Picture this: people will actually turn around and go home to get their phones if they forget them. People practically sleep with their phones. And yes, I've heard people using their mobile phones in public bathrooms. I don't quite get the mechanics of how everything works there, but it happens. Mobile phones are always on, always with you and specific to one particular owner.

What does this mean? If you can communicate with a customer via their mobile phone, your message is going to get through. In fact, if this communication is a text message, almost 100% of text messages are read and over 90% of them are read within 15 minutes. This is AMAZING!!

An important caveat needs to be mentioned here. Text messaging can only, ONLY, be done with permission from the owner of the phone. Marketing with text messages is 100% permission based. No Spam Allowed! Period. End of story.

Five Key Secrets to a Winning Formula

The ability to communicate through text messaging has created a new channel for businesses to engage customers, called mobile marketing. Many of you already use television, radio or print advertising. I'll show you why you should add mobile marketing to the mix.

In order to be successful in carrying out mobile marketing campaigns, there are several key strategies you must incorporate into what you're doing.

Key One – Create Irresistible, Compelling Offers

The first critical step you need to do when doing mobile marketing is getting permission from your customers. How do you get permission to do mobile marketing? You do this by extending an invitation to people. What am I talking about? You create a compelling, absolutely irresistible offer that people can't help but respond to.

You ask potential customers to text a word to a phone number in anticipation of getting something wonderful from your business in return. In geek speak, people would text a Keyword (a word) to a Short Code (a short phone number). This is called "opting in."

If they're going to give up their personal phone number and give their permission to receive messages from you, it will need to be for a very good reason. You must provide something of value that customers will want. You want them to drop what they're doing to text in for your offer. The text reply that is received from your business could be a coupon, a discount, a free offer, important information or news about an event. The possibilities are endless – but they must provide value.

Here are the benefits of obtaining this permission. Customers will have expressed an interest in receiving your text marketing messages and the result is that they look forward to your messages because of the value you're sending them in those messages. Your messages need to be important and meaningful to your customers in order for them to continue to want to receive your messages. Your customers always have the option of deciding they don't want to receive any more text messages from your business and they can terminate the relationship they have with you – at any time (this is called opting-out).

Key Two - Choose Simple, Relevant Keywords

You are asking people to text something to a phone number, often when they're on the run. They may sometimes have to remember the keyword and short code until they can get on their phone. You want to choose a keyword that is easy to spell, relevant to the offer, short to type and easy to remember.

Key Three - Integrate Mobile Campaigns Into All Your Marketing Activity

Let's say you own a restaurant. You serve steak, seafood and pasta dishes. You are open for lunch and dinner, seven days a week. You typically advertise to your local geographic area using some or all of the following traditional means.

- A billboard ad
- Direct mail postcards
- Table tents
- A radio ad
- Newspaper ads
- On your website
- On signage on your store window and in the store
- Signage in the street

You're basically marketing shotgun style, spraying your bullets everywhere and hoping to hit someone. You know you're hitting some targets but you can't always identify which marketing message the bullets came from.

With mobile marketing, you basically "marry" text message marketing together with these traditional marketing methods. You integrate a text message invitation into all your current marketing campaigns that you already carry out, such as:

"Text APPETIZER to 12345 and receive a Free Appetizer with Purchase of an Entrée."

If you use different keywords, you will be able to track which marketing method the responses came from. You will therefore know which marketing methods are working better than others or perhaps not working at all. Based on the results over time, you may decide to reallocate your marketing funds and/or save money by discontinuing ineffective marketing. You will be able to create more effective marketing strategies because now you can track results.

Key Four - Get to Know Your Customers

Now, at the same time you're finding out what's working with your advertising, you're also building a list of phone numbers from customers who have expressed an interest in your business' products or services.

With mobile marketing, you can begin to know more about your customers – who they are, what they like and want, and how they behave. There are several different types or styles of campaigns that are used with mobile marketing that can help you do this.

For example, a voting text campaign could tell you:
- Which customers prefer steak vs. seafood

- Which customers prefer to eat out for lunch vs. for dinner
- Which customers prefer to eat out on weekdays vs. weekends
- And so on.

You would personalize your campaigns to your business' products or services. With the information you gather, you create "groups" of customers with similar preferences. And you can continue to refine your groups as much as you need to, eventually allowing you to laser focus your marketing campaigns.

Key Five – Personalize Your Offers and Provide Value to Your Customers

Armed with the knowledge you have about your customers in the example above, you can send steak coupons to those who prefer to eat steaks and seafood coupons to those who prefer to eat seafood. Lunch coupons to those who prefer to eat out for lunch and dinner coupons to those who prefer to eat out for dinner. You won't bother people with coupons they're not interested in receiving. You will be able to laser focus your offers based on what you know – not on what you're guessing. Your offers must be something of value to your customers – a financial value, an informational value or a time-sensitive value.

I think you can guess the results of this type of marketing. If close to 100% of your texts are opened and the offer is aligned with that person's expressed preferences and of high value to them, there is an increased likelihood that this customer will take advantage of the offers you send her. Actual results from using mobile campaigns have shown there is an exceptionally high conversion for mobile offers compared to print or internet offers. If you think about it, this makes sense since your message is getting read and your message is truly targeted and personalized.

Mobile marketing can be used for an extensive array of business niches. Start with A and move on to Z and you'll cover them all. I'm sure your head is starting to spin right now with ideas swirling around about how to use mobile marketing.

I'll summarize my message and some marketing statistics for you.

- As of December 2010, there were 302.9 million mobile subscriptions in the U.S.A., 96% of the population.

- The majority of the population that owns a mobile phone has it with them all the time, the phone is always on and the phone belongs to one person.
- Almost 100% of mobile phones can send and receive text messages.
- SMS is the king of mobile marketing. Eight trillion text messages will be sent in 2011.
- Almost 100% of text messages are opened and read, more than 90% of them within 15 minutes.
- Text messages can, over time, become extremely targeted marketing messages, resulting in exceptionally high conversion rates.

You now have the Five Key Secrets to Winning with Mobile Marketing. If you use them, what's the result of successful mobile marketing campaigns?

- Increased Customer Traffic: As a business owner, once you've started the conversation using mobile marketing, you can encourage your current customers to come in more often to shop or to use your services.
- Increased Transaction Value: You can encourage your current customers to spend more each time they come in.

- Increased Customer Base: Your business will acquire more customers.
- Wash, rinse and repeat.

And isn't this what all business owners want? More customers, more sales and higher value sales.

So, Let's Start Mobile Marketing!

Of course, what I have presented here is only a basic introduction to mobile marketing for businesses and there is certainly much more information to be shared about this. I should also point out that mobile marketing includes more than just text message marketing. Other tools in the mobile marketing bag include ensuring you have a mobile ready website, using mobile ads, QR codes, mobile apps, and mobile loyalty programs. But I digress and these are certainly topics for future publications.

My goal has been to enlighten you with the incredible power text message marketing has for enabling local businesses to communicate with their customer base, form relationships and grow their bottom line.

There may be some of you who are still skeptical about this

newfangled mobile thing. Do you remember way back when you were wondering if your business needed one of those website things? Do you remember when you were wondering if your business needed an internet presence? You may be one of those business owners who were behind the eight ball and playing catch up by the time you realized that yes, indeed, you did need those things.

This time around, you need to be at the forefront of a powerful marketing movement. The time is now! You can't afford to be left behind. Remember, your competitors, who ran with that internet thing before you did? They are likely to be right up front with this mobile thing also and you'll be playing catch up again. That is, if you're still in business.

Don't hesitate another moment about using Mobile Marketing. Mobile Marketing is the future. Get on board!

ABOUT BLANCHE

For several years, Blanche Hayden has been helping local business owners to not only stay in business through these troubling economic times, but to grow their businesses, using local internet marketing strategies. More recently, Blanche realized the growing importance of incorporating mobile marketing strategies and has become a mobile marketing expert.

Blanche has a Doctorate in Organic Chemistry and a Masters in School Counseling. At different times in her life, she also acquired licenses in real estate, insurance and securities. She has been the founder and owner of several businesses herself, in an entrepreneurial role. Along the way, she came to the realization that without effective marketing, businesses will struggle to survive, much less grow and prosper. Her extremely diverse life's path has led Blanche to her current role as a Marketing Consultant to small businesses. She enjoys forming long-lasting relationships with her customers and helping them to be successful in their own chosen way.

Blanche is the co-author of several scientific articles in journals in the chemical industry and she is the happy wife of her husband, Glenn, and mother to their combined brood of five grown children and a very loving kitty cat.

You can find out more about Blanche and her marketing at: www.FindYourBizLocally.com.

You can contact Blanche at info@findyourbizlocally.com or 832-381-7830.

CHAPTER 7

CAN YOU ANSWER THESE 5 CRUCIAL QUESTIONS ABOUT YOUR BUSINESS TO MAKE PEOPLE BUY?

By Louie Lambrianidis

Introduction

Why should people buy from your business? What makes your business so special compared to every other business competing with yours? And why should prospects even care?

We live in a world where we experience indifferent mediocrity every day from businesses that just don't get it. Many businesses claim to be better and different than their competitors, but we find them to be similar or even the same in some cases. We talk to similar people, with similar qualifications selling us things we don't want or need. We even see similar products, services, and prices, and silently wish businesses would stop boring us and excite us with much more.

Whether intentional or not, such businesses force us to reduce our buying decision to just one dimension; who has the lowest price. And when we focus on who has the lowest price, there can only be one business in your area who is first to offer it. We are never told about any other value proposition that we should take into account for our benefit. It is assumed that we know.

The point is that as a business owner, you need to purposefully position your business and offers differently in the mind of people compared to your competitor to really standout. By standing out, you give people compelling reasons to buy from your business. By communicating and promoting these reasons, you influence people's emotions to buy from you instead of your competitors.

To make people buy, you must be able to discover qualities buyers think about, look for, and express in making their buying decision. To discover these qualities for your business, there are 5 crucial questions about your business you must be able to answer with a deeper insight and understanding than your competitors. When you do understand the qualities that buyers look for, and tell them you have them, you can influence them to buy immediately.

Question 1. What specific problems and challenges does your local business solve for people?

People buy based on their needs and wants. When they have problems, they look for solutions. Does your business just peddle products and\or services, or does it focus on offering solutions to problems that people have?

Retailers today tend to just be order takers. They don't engage with customers. They just take and process the order. Some retailers even treat customers with disdain by ignoring them altogether. Businesses that understand how their products and services help to solve real problems will always perform better than those that just take orders.

So as a business owner, ask yourself the following questions:

- What specific problems do each of my products and

services solve for customers?

- What specific challenges do my products and services help people overcome?

When thinking about problems and challenges people have, think about the following 5 basic needs that motivate people to buy:

1. Importance – people want to feel superior.
2. Appreciated – people want to be recognized and respected.
3. Liked – people seek and want the approval of others to feel validated.
4. Convenience – people want things to be easy to attain instant gratification.
5. Success – people want success in what is important to them whether it be finances, relationships, career, or health.

By understanding how your products and services can fulfill any or all of these basic needs, it allows you to address the underlying motives the buyer has in solving their problems and challenges. This makes it easier for you to position your products and services as the best solution to satisfy those needs.

Question 2. Why do prospects and customers come to your local business instead of your competitors?

This may seem like an obvious question to ask, but it is surprising how many business owners cannot answer it with a high degree of confidence. They second guess but never take the time to survey their prospects or customers to really find out. What is more disturbing is that business owners expend very little effort in doing any competitor analysis and hence don't even know how they are different in their local market.

In the absence of any difference of value to offer prospects, people will focus on price alone and when they focus on price alone, they look for the business that offers the lowest price. If your business is not the price leader, then you will not get the sale! But you can only have one price leader for each category of product and service, and you don't want to be the price leader if the margins are very slim and the volume of transactions unpredictable.

It is better to find out why your prospects and customers come to your business instead of your competitors, and use that information in all your marketing to attract more of them. Communicate this to your prospects and customers at every opportunity to reinforce it in their minds so they sense an affinity with your business.

Question 3. What makes your local business, products, and services better than your competitors?

Another important question to answer is why your business, products, and services are better than your competitors. What is it specifically that makes them better and why should a prospect or customer care? Is it the price, the service, the delivery, the durability, the exclusivity, the convenience, the availability, the warranty, the expertise, the product features, or some other combination that makes your business stand out amongst the competition? McDonalds™ doesn't make the best hamburgers in the world, but they do make them exactly the same around the world and you can find one in most cities too! The benefit of consistency and accessibility is used by McDonalds™ to differentiate themselves in the mind of the consumer from their competitors.

Identify who your competitors are in your local area or region and study and analyze them regularly so you can be at least one step ahead of them at every turn in the market place. Look closely at their advertising, website, shop front, and signage. Does anything stand out that will resonate with consumers? Do they use special offers? How do they attract prospects? Learn as much as you can and look for ways to be different and better so your business stands out.

Question 4. What benefits do your customers enjoy that they can't get anywhere else in your local area?

Selling a product on its own is not enough to sustain business growth for the long term. You must wrap your product and services up with benefits that <u>can't</u> be found elsewhere easily. Does your business offer tips and advice on how to use your products and services to get the best value out of them? Can you show or demonstrate the benefits to customers so they can enjoy rapid satisfaction with their purchase? Can you reinforce that they made the best decision in dealing with your business? Do your products and services come with a solid guarantee to eliminate all perceived risks the prospect or customer has?

Do you have a follow up process to help customers really get usage and value from their purchase? Do you have a loyalty program for customers to show them you really care and want them to come back and get even more value?

Find ways to extend the benefits you customers can enjoy beyond the initial transaction and your business will be rewarded with more new business.

Question 5. What deals can you offer prospects and returning customers to entice them to buy instantly?

Understanding how to position your business key strengths to craft enticing deals is just as important in helping people buy from you. Prospects and customers love special deals and want to be the first to hear about them. Designing incentives and offers doesn't need to be complex. Just be creative and keep them simple to understand. Offer something of value and let people know.

So many businesses treat their customers as a single transaction and never give them a reason to return and buy more. How difficult is it to offer a simple discount coupon to be redeemed with their next purchase?

It costs 10 times more in time and effort to find a new customer than it does to sell to an existing customer. Why? Because you have already invested the time and effort to establish a relationship in getting their first purchase. They already know, like, and trust you and your business otherwise they would not buy from you. So always have offers ready for new prospects and existing customers. Don't push your offers on them with a hard sell, but make them aware of it in a non-threatening way during your conversation. At best they will buy what you have on offer, at worse they will pass up the offer but thank you for it.

Conclusion

Spending time to answer the 5 crucial questions above about your business will set up your business so that people want to buy. Furthermore, they will want to buy from you and your business instead of your competitors because you understand and communicate points of difference and highlight benefits at the core of their motives.

But you don't stop there. You follow up with your customers to ensure they are getting value from using your products and services. And finally, you make enticing offers that are hard to pass up and you make them often to continue to build on the relationship with your existing customers.

The use and result of such insights will help your business to grow a base of satisfied and loyal customers that will sustain your local business for the long term.

CHAPTER 8

HOW TO CREATE FREE PUBLICITY FOR YOUR LOCAL BUSINESS IN AS LITTLE AS FIVE DAYS

By Louie Lambrianidis

Introduction

If your local business is not well known in your local area, it is time to give it a boost with some FREE publicity to make your business stand out from your local competition.

Writing simple articles and publishing them online, is like having a silent salesperson working for your business around the clock non-stop. Articles not only promote your business, but they give it valuable credibility, especially when your business is not well known.

Opportunities for free publicity abound, especially in local areas. With so many different types of online and offline

111

media hungry for new content, you can't fail to get exposure for your business. It isn't as difficult as you might think.

Here are 5 article marketing strategies for generating free online and offline publicity for your local business for the long term.

You will discover:

1. The 4 specific "evergreen" benefits articles will provide your business
2. The 7 simple steps to writing brilliant articles that get noticed
3. How to find publishers who are eager to publish your articles
4. Three additional ways to get more free publicity with your articles
5. Where to find affordable help with creating articles if you don't like writing

The purpose here is to give you a proven and easy to follow roadmap for generating all the free publicity your business can handle with simple articles you can create and publish in as little as 5 days.

Enduring Benefits Published Articles Provide Your Business

People use search engines such as Google™, Yahoo™, and Bing™, to search and find answers to their questions every day. Search engines feed off content by indexing it. This indexing is mainly automated by using proprietary software or by teams of human editors who review and categorize content. In fact, Google™ uses highly complex rules to assess the quality of published content on web sites. If your content is high quality, your web site will eventually enjoy a higher ranking and more people will see it.

Irrespective of how content is indexed, people use search engines to look for helpful information. They want to find and buy products and services, preferably in their local area, and they want quality advice and information to help them make good buying decisions.

Where does this quality information come from? One source is from people who publish quality articles about products and services. The articles can be full blown reviews with pros and cons, or short recommendations based on the experience of using a product or service.

People searching for your locally offered products and services are more likely to find you and make contact. For example, if someone is searching for "car servicing," and your business offers car tuning services, you can write a short article on the best car oil for car engines. In the article, you explain why your business replaces all car oils with "Castrol™ Magnatec Professional Premium Car Engine Oil," highlighting fuel cost savings as a key benefit. At the end of the article include a short profile of your business so your readers can contact you. This ensures that your business becomes known for using the best car engine oil with every car tuning service.

People also search for well-known brand name products or services that your business offers. Your articles can also reach people who are searching for those brand names. In the example above, the brand name "Castrol™ Magnatec Professional Premium Car Engine Oil" may be widely advertised on offline media such as roadside billboards. In the article, you have already made the connection between the product brand name and the fact that your business uses that product as part of every car service. So someone who is prompted by a local billboard to search for the brand name product, may indirectly also find out about your business and book in a car service because they know you use that specific brand name product.

Publishing articles online also creates keyword or website focused backlinks. These links help boost your article's exposure online through syndication. Google™ uses the number of backlinks to an article as one indicator of high quality content when indexing content.

Writing and publishing articles on topics that are centered on the core knowledge of your local business also makes you the local expert. This form of free publicity gives your business more credibility than your competitors who are not using articles to promote their business locally. In the next section I will outline the simple steps to writing quality articles.

7 Steps to Writing Articles that Give Your Business Instant Credibility

So what is involved in writing articles? Here are the 7 simple steps for creating highly effective articles:

1.   Choose topics centered on the specific knowledge your business offers to help people make good purchasing decisions. For example, if you are in the

business of car engine tuning services, a relevant article topic would be "How to Choose a Fuel Efficient Car Engine Oil for Your Car."

2. Write articles that speak directly to your "ideal customer," keeping a vision of this type of person firmly in mind as you write. For example, if your ideal customer is a middle aged family man who wants to save on motoring costs, then educate him about how the right car engine oil can help fathers with a young family to get more mileage from their family sedan and save them money.

3. Capture the attention of your ideal customer and appeal to their emotions with a powerful article title that stands out. For example, "How Fathers on a Tight Budget Can Save $300 by Using a Fuel Efficient Car Engine Oil in their Family Car."

4. Select a highly focused, long-tailed keyword phrase (3 words or more) that is used by people searching for your products or services. Use it in your headline and the first paragraph of your article while making it sound conversational. For example, the keyword phrase "fuel efficient car engine oil" is a long tailed key phrase that can be used in the title and throughout the article in sentences. Don't use the same keyword phrase more than 2 times in the body

of your article otherwise you will devalue the quality of the article.

5.   At the end of the article, create an author's Resource Box that has your name, your business name, and a strong call to action with a link to entice the reader to click through to your website or landing page on your website. If you don't have a website, then use your business phone and fax number or other offline contact details. For example, offer the reader a free 11 Point Car Safety Check, or a free car engine oil check and top up as an inducement for them to take action to visit your local business.

6.   Submit your articles, along with your author Resource Box and any other relevant information such as your business details to top Article Directories. Publishers of Article Directories are always looking for good quality articles to be listed in their directories.

7.   Create and submit three 400-600 word articles to the top Article Directories online in the first 5 days and then one new article every week for at least 3 months to build your business reputation online and in your local area. Publishing articles has a cumulative benefit in getting free publicity for your business. The more articles you publish and the

more regularly you publish them, the greater the exposure and publicity for your business.

How to Find Top Article Directories to Publish Your Articles

To publish your articles for maximum exposure, submit them to top article directories on the web. Article Directories look for article submissions on all sorts of topics. Articles are collated under subject categories to make it easier for people to find them in the article directory. Articles written by authors who want to share their knowledge and expertise use Article Directories to raise their profile, credibility, and to obtain free exposure for their business.

Top Article Directories also have quality guidelines that must be achieved before an article is accepted and published on an article directory. Some guidelines set the quality standard at a low level, while others set the level high. Most top Article Directories will provide specific feedback on how to improve the quality of your article if it does not meet the minimum quality standard described in their guidelines.

Search engines like Google™, love to index top Article Directories because articles generally provide higher quality content and focus on a very specific topic of interest to the reader. So how do you find top article directories that take article submissions? You just search for "article directories" using Google™ and you will find many to choose from. Three of the top article directories to submit your articles to include: www.ezinearticles.com, www.articlebase.com, and www.goarticles.com.

There are many other Article Directories, but the ones above have been around a long time and perform well at getting you exposure online. Visit these articles directories and have a look at articles others have published on your subject or topic to become familiar with what others before you have done. Look for the author's Resource Box to get an idea of what is expected. Also read the author guidelines which provide helpful advice for first time authors and sign up for a free account.

Three Ways to Reuse Your Articles to Get Even More Free Publicity

Articles can also be repurposed to provide your business with even more free publicity. Once you have your articles published in an article directory, here are 3 additional ways to use your articles for extra publicity and exposure:

1. Make minor changes to the title and the content of the article so that the article is still on topic but is a variation of the original article. Then submit these articles to other top Article Directories that you have not used.

2. After your articles have been published for 30-days, check to see how many people have viewed your articles (most article directories offer this information). If you have had more than 100 views of any article, then send a copy of your article to the editors of the business section of your local newspapers and ask them to interview you about your article topic.

3. Most local business groups have a newsletter they send to their members on a regular basis. Contact these groups and offer your articles as free content they can use in their newsletter.

There are many other ways to repurpose and reuse the content of your articles. Never stop at just a single submission to one article directory, especially if the topic is interesting and the article is well written and offers valuable advice.

Where to Find Affordable Help to Create Your Articles

If you want to use articles to promote your business but feel you are not a confident article writer, then you can hire an article writer to help you. Article writers typically charge between $5 and $50 per article depending on the length of the article, the time spent on doing any research, and the time spent on proof reading and corrections. To find article writers, do a search on Google™. Also do a search on "review of article writing services" to find article writing services others have used and reviewed.

Before hiring an article writer, make sure you review at least one sample of their work and ask them if they charge extra for rework if you are not satisfied with the quality of their first draft. Also make sure that you have the full rights and ownership to the articles to use them in any way you want.

Most writers also like to be hired to write a "pack of articles" and offer a discount on multiple articles. Buying a pack of 5 or 10 articles gives you more content to choose from and use in promoting your business.

You can also request that your articles be search engine optimized (SEO) by supplying the writer with specific keywords and keyword phrases related to your business, your products, and services. If you want your article to have a local focus, then also use the name of the city and\or country from which your business operates in your article. For example, "Melbourne Car Tuning Services Australia" or "Houston Texas Car Tuning Services" are all locally focused keyword phrases.

Conclusion

Creating and publishing simple 400-600 word articles that offer readers helpful and valuable information and advice, is a proven way to get your local business noticed online and offline. The key to getting free publicity with articles is to use and reuse the content in different ways on a regular basis. It is not difficult to write about topics in which your business specializes in, even if you think you can't write. People trust local business owners who offer their advice and expertise to help them solve their problems. Don't let the fear of writing stop you. Hire an article writer to do the heavy writing for you and spend your time reviewing the quality of their work.

Follow the advice above to get your local business FREE publicity in as little as 5 days and more exposure to people who are looking for your products and services in your local area.

ABOUT LOUIE

Louie Lambrianidis helps businesses grow fast. He is a Local Internet Marketing Expert and Business Consultant based in Melbourne Australia. He works directly with business owners to design and implement proven online and offline marketing strategies that get results.

Business owners looking for a professional leader and coach to help them grow their business, seek out Louie. With over 20 years of professional experience in technology, management, and business, and formal qualifications including an MBA, Louie's practical insights guarantees results fast.

Louie has been responsible for delivering successful projects and consulting assignments from across industry sectors that include, financial services, utilities, government, IT services, construction, and manufacturing. He is a trusted advisor and leader of change and innovation in helping businesses to identify and fully utilize their marketing and technology assets to achieve and sustain growth.

Marketing and technology assets that are not working for your business are just another wasted resource costing you money. Louie uses his step by step Hidden Marketing and Technology Asset System to create tailored marketing strategies that are implemented and supported with technology to grow any business. This unique business strategy mix of marketing and technology assets is so effective that it enables even small local businesses to grow exponentially!

To discover more about the benefits of Local Internet Marketing for your business and how Louie can help you grow your business, visit
www.StepByStepBusinessGrowth.com
and get your FREE copy of "Unlimited Profitable Customers for Local Business Owners."

CHAPTER 9

THINK STRATEGY: IT'S NOT ABOUT THE WEBSITE

By Mark Eland

Have you ever seen a new business open up in your town only to see it close just a short while later? Why do you think that is? The building was appealing, the signage was eye catching and attractive and there were a few cars in the parking lot, but for some reason the business just didn't make it.

My guess is the business didn't have a strong marketing strategy in place to sustain any initial business they might have attracted.

This same scenario is played out every day online by local businesses.

A typical conversation with a local business owner might go something like this:

"How's your business doing online?"

"Really well. We launched our new web site last quarter. It's pretty flashy, and everyone seems to like it."

Sound familiar? It's interesting that when business owners, sales managers, and salespeople talk about Internet strategy, they always want to focus on what their web site looks like. What if I told you that it's not about how your web site looks? After all, how many customers and prospects are going there, anyway – and how many other "spiffy," flashy sites are they going to visit before and after yours?

The key to your Internet marketing strategy is not making your web site look good, but using the Internet to increase sales.

Implementing an effective Internet marketing strategy in order to increase your business's sales and revenues is not rocket science. Unfortunately, many Internet Marketing consultants tend to throw around jargon, statistics, and acronyms until your head is spinning and you think only technical geeks can understand Internet marketing.

In essence, they want to convince you that the true path to Internet marketing success is steep, complex, and costly. Fortunately, this is not the case.

In this chapter I'm going to cover a few key Internet marketing strategies that if applied by most local businesses they would be stunned by how much more business and revenue they could be bringing in.

Following these key concepts to generate an effective Internet marketing strategy will help your company improve in all areas of business:

#1 – Generate as Much Targeted Traffic to Your Business as Possible

If you have a web site, it's not about how fancy it is but how effective it is. From a marketing standpoint, the general purpose of a web site is for prospects that don't know you to find out about you and take an action to call you, leave their email address, or come to your place of business. But if no one can find your business that doesn't already know your company's name, there's little point. This seems obvious, but there are many businesses that obviously spent a lot of money creating their fancy web site, and you can't even find their business on a search engine.

Fortunately, getting your business to come up at the top of search engines is probably not as difficult as you think. The great thing about search engines is that once your business is listed high on the search results, you get absolutely free leads.

In a nutshell, here are four ways to increase your number of targeted visitors.

1. Increase your number of websites

You should not think about your web *site* (singular). Too many Internet marketers are preoccupied with the design of their single site's home page when they should be using their time and energy to create *multiple* web sites.

Why not post web sites focusing on the specific needs of your target market to maximize your visitor and lead potential. By doing so you increase the potential of having more listings and more opportunities to be discovered in the search engines.

2. Increase your website's rankings in the free search engines

The power of search engines can't be underestimated, and any business with real overhead and revenues should take their power seriously. Search Engine Optimization (SEO), which increases your rankings on search engines, is both an art and a science.

The good news is that getting your business listed high in the search engines is not rocket science. Indeed, you can outsource the optimization of your web site(s) for search engines, but you can also do it yourself.

3. Increase the online marketing of your business

There are many excellent, and cost-effective, ways to increase the visibility of your business, and increase traffic to your web site. A few examples include:

- Google Places
- Online ads
- Directories
- Web 2.0 sites
- Reviews

- E-mail newsletters (yours and/or others)
- Newsgroups

4. Increase the offline marketing of your website

Consider going offline to attract online visitors. If this sounds like a step backwards, it is actually anything but. The key to an integrated marketing strategy is just that – to *integrate* all of your online and offline marketing initiatives into an overall cohesive strategy.

The process of "converting" offline marketing and advertising into online interactive marketing prospects allows you to build your database of prospects and begin more relationships, more quickly. The idea is to promote not only your business but your web site(s) offline, and produce maximum lead generation for your interactive communication system.

#2 - Capture as Many Leads as Possible

You can look at any number of web sites and immediately realize that they are not capturing as many leads as possible – because most are not capturing *any* leads. The site designers may have had lengthy discussions about the placement of the navigation, or the home page colors, or the copy, but they are still just swinging blind, because they don't understand what they're supposed to be swinging at.

The reason so many web sites miss the point of their very existence is that the usually savvy businesspeople who build them are looking at the web site from the wrong perspective. They see a web site as simply another vehicle for outmoded one-way communication – not as an interactive tool.

If you look at a web site as just another marketing tool you're missing the point. You're only doing what 80-90 percent of existing web sites are already doing and in so doing, you are wasting or ignoring an enormous reserve of untapped marketing and sales potential.

#3 - Manage the Content of Your Websites Yourself

You know the old saying: "If you want something done right, do it yourself." Well, that applies to your web site, too. Planning how to manage the content of your web site should be a component of your Internet marketing strategy.

It used to be that unless you were a computer geek, you had to rely on IT people to change your web site content – which meant relying on their schedules, paying their prices, and trusting their instincts, which weren't always correct.

But times have changed for the better and content management tools or software applications now enable nonprogrammers to make changes to their own web sites, or at least update selected pages of the site. It doesn't do a company's interactive marketing efforts much good to run a cool new promotion which is over by the time the web developer finds the time to update the site.

In short, you need the ability to publish web pages to support your marketing or sales efforts whenever you need or want, you would be crazy not to.

Some effective examples of these materials might include:

- Special discount offers – sending a link to qualified, steady or large customers only
- Coupons with short expiration windows – to encourage the customer to act quickly

- Customer surveys – e-mail a link and award a bonus to those who click in and complete the survey

When you have content management capabilities, you will be amazed at the number of great marketing ideas that will spring to mind. On the other hand, if you don't have this ability, you probably won't be thinking about all the ways you can keep in touch with your customers.

#4 - Use a Sequential Auto-Responder

If you have not used this powerful tool before, prepare yourself. It will skyrocket your sales.

Generally, an auto-responder refers to an e-mail program that automatically replies each time it receives an e-mail. For instance, when you e-mail a company and immediately receive a reply reading, "Thank you for your interest in XYZ Company. We will do our best to get back to you within 24-48 hours," that's the work of an auto-responder program.

The concept of the auto-responder has been around for quite a while, and the technology is not rocket science, but few businesses are taking advantage of this tool in the right way. That's unfortunate, because when used properly and consistently, auto-responder e-mail provides a huge potential for growth.

The great advantage of the *sequential* auto-responder is that it allows you to send a series of data-driven (personalized) e-mails to prospects on a pre-set schedule. Imagine if no prospect ever "slipped through the cracks." Imagine being able to follow up with 100 percent of your prospects, 100 percent of the time. That's what happens when you properly utilize a sequential auto-responder.

#5 - Use a Group Email Program to Keep in Touch with All Your Prospects and Customers

Consider all the possibilities and benefits of using data driven emails to build relationships with your customers and prospects through electronic communications, and the good ideas will just keep coming.

For example:

- Do you have overstocked inventory? For the cost of an e-mail, and much less time than doing markdowns or Returns to Vendor, you can take pictures of the merchandise, paste them in an e-mail with descriptions and prices, and send it to all your customers.

- Did your Bed & Breakfast get a bunch of cancellations for the weekend, and you need to fill some of those empty rooms? Time to run a Weekend Special! Take a few minutes to create an e-mail and send it out to everyone in your database.

- Do you have customers who haven't bought anything in a while? Make them an offer they can't refuse by sending out a special discount coupon they can print from their computer and redeem at the store. Better yet, electronically deposit "funds" on their gift cards and send an e-mail inviting them to spend the "free money" they'll get if they come in by a deadline you set.

The possibilities are as numerous as your business needs.

#6 - Leverage Social Media Networks

Local businesses that are rushing to get involved in social media need to realize that including social media in your marketing strategy is a long-term commitment to change, don't expect overnight results.

Social Media is about listening and responding to what customers are saying about your business and its products and services. Social media can supply good intelligence and give your company a chance to interact with customers.

Any company that isn't willing to listen to customers and be nimble and quick enough to respond, and, when necessary, change, will soon be unable to compete with smart, tech-savvy companies that can turn on a dime.

Outline your social media strategy and support your strategy with tactics. Without a carefully thought-out plan, you'll eventually be overwhelmed with social media and even worse, get burned out by it.

In a nutshell, this is a combination of modern technology and good business techniques. Once you implement these concepts and start mapping out your marketing strategy for increasing communications with your customers and prospects, the magic begins and I think you will be amazed at the results.

ABOUT MARK

Mark Eiland is the founder of BizBeFound LLC, a boutique internet marketing firm in Austin, Texas providing its clients with tailored solutions to marketing strategies that generate new business and increase revenue through the power of the Internet.

Mark has been running his own eCommerce businesses on the Internet since 2006. In 2010, Mark left a 30+ year corporate career where he was an IT manager for companies such as Bank of America and IBM and founded BizBeFound with a passion for working with small businesses.

Mark takes a strategic approach to getting his client's products and services findable on the Internet. Having a business website findable is a good thing but why stop there? Why not have multiple paths leading customers to find and buy the products and services a business has to offer?

Mark's passion and straight forward approach to Internet marketing has allowed him to help many small businesses experience success online for the first time.

Mark Eiland, Founder
BizBeFound.com
business@bizbefound.com
512-219-0306 (Phone)
888-346-4509 (Toll Free)

CHAPTER 10
REEL THEM IN WITH PPC

By Heather Stewart

If you're a small business owner, the internet is both a blessing and curse. On one hand, you can have a presence on the web that informs and engages your customers, providing a 24 hours a day, 7 days a week advertising service.

On the other hand, because everyone from massive corporations to your Aunt Sally is on the web, it can be really difficult to get anyone to notice your site. Having a web presence and an internet advertising strategy is not a Field of Dreams situation; just because you build it doesn't mean they'll come.

But it is possible to reach people on the internet. In fact, it's entirely possible to get all the traffic that you want to your website and show up at the top of every search. This is what Pay Per Click advertising, or PPC, is all about.

What is PPC?

When you Google something, what you usually get are one to three short ads at the top of the page, and a handful of them on the right side. They look more or less like the regular search results, and they are the source of Google's billions. These are pay per click ads.

If you click on one of them, you're taken to the website of the advertiser, and Google charges them a fee for the click. Basically, the advertiser is paying for Google to send them traffic to their website, in hopes of monetizing the traffic.

This is the essence of PPC, which is exactly what it sounds like: you're paying for clicks. Google is far from the only company doing it, either, and you can pay for traffic from Yahoo, Bing and Facebook, amongst countless others.

Pros and Cons of PPC

Like anything else in business, there are pros and cons to using PPC.

PROS

- The amount of traffic you can get to your website is limited only by your budget

- You can track your ROI with incredible precision
- You don't need to be technical wizard to do it
- Traffic is instant, rather than waiting for your website to move up in the search engines

CONS

- Can be expensive, especially when you're learning
- Requires constant and consistent monitoring
- Requires that your website be optimized for capturing and retain customers
- Works better for some business models than others
- PPC is an amazingly flexible and powerful advertising tool, but it's also one that can require a lot of time to master. Putting an ad in the local newspaper or billboard space can be expensive, but it's a fairly straightforward process. PPC advertising requires you to test and test and test some more, or hire someone who will, to get the maximum benefit from it.

How to Make PPC Work for Your Business

The very first thing you need to use PPC is a web presence. This doesn't have to be a website in the traditional sense, since you can use things like a Facebook fan page or a blog, but you absolutely need to have a place where you can send the people clicking on your ad.

Ideally, you want to have something for them to buy or something you're giving away in return for their email addresses. You want to be able to retain them as a customer and build a relationship, not just have them glance at your site and click the back button.

So if, for example, you're using PPC to advertise your Italian restaurant, you could have a webpage that has your hours, the menu and some contact information, but what would be ideal is to offer potential customers a ten percent discount in exchange for their email address.

This improves your ROI in two ways; one, the person who has a ten percent discount is a lot more likely to actually visit the restaurant and two, you can contact them again with special incentives.

The next thing you need to do is decide what keywords you want your ad to show up for. In PPC, you create a group of keywords that when searched for, triggers your ad to show up. If you're selling shoes, for instance, you might want to have your ad appear when someone searches for Louboutin or Nike or Timberland.

The best to get started at finding keywords for your PPC ad campaign is to put yourself in the mind of your customer. If you were looking for whatever it is that your business does or sales, what you search for. Try to write down a list of these, and don't be afraid to be silly or obscure.

Once you do, go to Google's Keyword Tool, which allows you to see how many times word is searched for and gives you a bunch of suggestions, and start loading the words in. This will give you a handle on how many people are searching for those keywords, as well as giving you a bunch more keywords to consider.

The goal is to come up with a group of keywords that will give a broad target for your PPC campaign. At the early stages, more is probably better, although you might want to just try for the fifty or so best words.

One thing to keep in mind is that if your business doesn't actually sell things online, which is the case for restaurants and nearly any service business, you want to try and limit the clicks you're paying for to your geographic area. One way to do that is to simply add the name of your city in front of the keywords, although this is not the best way to do it.

After you have the keywords, you need to create brief, compelling ads. How long these are going to be will depend on the PPC advertising platform, but they generally run two short sentences or so. You will need to create more than one, so that you can test and tweak.

You will also need to set a daily budget and an overall budget. If you're doing this on your own, you need to be prepared to spend money on learning; your first campaigns are not likely to be homeruns. You might want to balance this against the cost of hiring someone to manage your campaign for you and decide which makes more sense for your business.

Once you've done all that, you can sign up as advertiser with one of the companies offering PPC advertising. Google is the dominant force in the field, but it may actually be better to go with a smaller, and therefore less expensive, company like Yahoo to begin with, so that you can get the most out of your budget.

All of them will require you to bid on keywords, where you

basically tell them how much per click you are willing to pay to get your ad seen. As you might imagine, the less you bid, the further down the page your ad will appear.

How much you can expect to pay depends entirely on the keyword and the competition. Some keywords will cost you five dollars for each click, and some will cost a penny. Always try to get the most clicks for your daily budget.

After your ads start running, you need to monitor which ads and keywords are producing and which aren't. What you want to do is test and tweak until you've found the combination the produces the results you are looking for, and then start scaling those campaigns up.

This is a trial and error process, so your ROI is going to be back loaded; once you find profitably campaigns, you can make a lot of money, but you may lose money in the early stages.

One thing that most PPC advertising programs now offer is geo-targeting, which means that your ads will only appear to people searching within the area you want. This is absolutely key to running a successful PPC campaign for small businesses, and it can dramatically cut cost, so make sure you are running campaigns only in the areas where your customers are.

Pay Per Click advertising can be a genuine game changer for many businesses, but you need to approach with a long term mindset and an eye towards building the business. If you can do that, PPC is a great tool for helping you make the most of whatever business you're in, from cutting hair to selling brake pads.

ABOUT HEATHER

Heather Stewart is an internet entrepreneur who is passionate about using proven internet marketing ideas to benefit the local business community.

Based on this passion, her evolving company, (Bionics Marketing), helps small and medium sized businesses develop a mix of online and traditional lead generation strategies that can make massive differences to sales revenues in their specific markets. She also assists local experts get their name and message out to the community.

Heather has been online since the early 90's. She keeps up with the rapidly changing market and current trends in lead generation and marketing by being active in internet forums and continuous investment in education on new methods. Heather resides in the Los Angeles area.

Contact Heather at:
www.bionicsmarketing.com

CHAPTER 11

REAL ESTATE MOBILE MARKETING

By Lonnie Stanley

If you are a realtor or a home owner trying to sell your own house and wanting ways to stand out from the crowd, mobile marketing is probably the answer you've been looking for. It puts information right in the hands of the potential buyer in ways never before thought possible. It really doesn't matter if you are a realtor or someone just trying to sell your own house, mobile marketing can bring buyers to your doorstep. Videos, pictures, specific information, location, all these things and more can be used in a mobile website to promote your house.

One of the major problems when trying to sell a home is contacting potential buyers who drive by and look at homes that are on the market. The options they currently have are: telephone and information sleeves. Most people looking for homes will not call and get an appointment, since they really do not want to talk to a salesperson. When they have enough information, they will usually call.

The other option currently used to give the potential buyer information on the house is by putting sleeves with sheets about the house in them on the realtor signs. This method never really gives the potential buyer enough information to make a decision about the house. The paper gives basic information and a frontal picture that really doesn't help. Also a problem with using the sleeves is that a lot of times they are empty. Whether the home owner forgot to fill it up or the neighborhood kids decided to remove them for you. Either way, the information was not always available.

The potential buyer can view the home in their local newspaper or real estate weekly, but getting to actually see inside the house is impossible unless they contact the realtor and set up an appointment.

Instant information was never really available until now. Since more than half of the phone users are carrying smart phones (or mobile devices), multiple ways of reaching potential buyers have been created. Some realtors have apps created for download to smart phones while others have used a more direct means of communication, through text messages and QR codes.

Mobile websites are becoming more and more common as people are away from their computers and using their phones to search the web. Smart phones have created opportunities to put instant information in the hands of potential buyers. QR codes enhance this ability by giving direct links to the mobile website (QR codes will be talked about later). Text messages aren't just for kids anymore. Texting has become a vital way to get information into the hands of customers and clients. Not only does it provide new information, but it can also be used to remind clients of appointments, so that you're not left standing in an empty house with no one to show it to.

I have worked with a local realtor to create an SMS campaign that allowed her to place set keywords on her signs that she could use over and over again. Combining an SMS campaign with a mobile website, can provide more information about the house as well as collect the phone number of the person. One thing that must be mentioned here is that when using an SMS messaging program, you must give information that they can "Opt Out" by replying "STOP".

Let's use this scenario, a potential buyer drives by a house and decides that he/she would like some more information. The realtor's sign states "Text Realtydemo to 72727 to see more information about this home." Eager to see how this was going to work, the potential buyer picks up the phone and texts the keyword to the number provided. In just a matter of seconds a reply pops into the message box. "From Realtor, thank you for your interest in this home. For more information click http://bit.ly/jNebyr and select browser (or internet)." Once the link is clicked, it will take them to the mobile website where additional information can be viewed.

Pictures, video, contact information, price, and location are now readily available anytime the buyer wants to take a look. An informed decision can now be made as to whether the buyer wants to schedule an appointment or to keep looking until they find something that suits them.

Since the buyer texted in, it gave the realtor the potential buyer's phone number, so that he/she can call back to see if their interest was in the home, the location, or the price range.

You can see how this works by texting "Realtydemo" to

72727 (type keyword into comment section of phone and then send it to "72727"). With our realtor, I set it up so that she would only have to make a few signs. She came up with several keywords that were generic in nature, but would allow her to know which home she was offering. By doing this, she could create her message boards and attach them to the realtor sign she placed in a seller's yard. As she sold a home, I would change the mobile website and SMS message to reflect the new home being offered. This eliminated additional cost to her for creating different signs.

The mobile website can have a page with the realtor's information and have his/her phone number as click to call. Click to Call allows the buyer to click on the phone number and have the number pull up on their phone. At which time all they have to do is place the call.

Another great option that can be placed on a webpage is a link to the address. When hyper-linked to Google's map, this selection can give the buyer the ability to get turn by turn directions to their phone.

 QR Codes (Quick Response) as seen here can be used with ads to give the potential buyer the ability to see the mobile website. It can also be embedded with a link to Google maps for directions, or can give basic information about the house.

This works really well and provides your potential buyer with all the information they need in order to make the decision to contact the realtor to schedule an appointment. QR codes can also be embedded with tracking to show what time of day and what days it was being used. This helps the realtor to know when the peak times are that people are looking at homes to buy.

Apps are another way Real Estate companies are moving into the mobile market. Though still new to some areas, some have had a good response to the apps. I'm not sure how many people would actually use the app if it only showed one Broker's listings. This may work for some areas, but I still feel the most direct approach works best. Interacting with potential buyers through a text message campaign or setting up appointments through a mobile platform is still the best option.

ABOUT LONNIE

Lonnie Stanley is a Local Mobile & Internet Marketing expert and small business consultant who works with businesses to make them findable on the internet and accessible through mobile platforms. Lonnie realizes that mobile marketing is the new paradigm in marketing with more consumers searching, shopping, and buying with mobile devices.

Lonnie teaches local businesses how to maximize their mobile presence by making sure they can be found when consumers are using their phones to search for local businesses. Lonnie emphasizes the importance of having Google Place Pages up to date as this is very important to the mobile consumer when they are ready to eat or make a purchase. Maintaining positive reviews can go a long way to helping a consumer, who is ready to buy, choose one business over another.

To learn more about Lonnie Stanley and receive up to date information by a leading expert in mobile marketing, visit www.LonnieAStanley.com.

CHAPTER 12

TRADITIONAL MARKETING IS DEAD! OR IS IT?

By Eric LeRiche

Introduction

It was a beautiful Sunday morning, my wife and I decided to bike to the local market to grab a nice light breakfast.

20 minutes later we were sitting down on a small terrace at an unpresumptuous restaurant overlooking a famous canal here in Montreal when I noticed on the place mat a QR code. For those who don't know what a QR Code is, "QR" means "Quick Reference" and looks like a bar code but square in shape.

 I don't want to get into the details of what a QR Code is apart from telling you that most smart phones have QR code reader which allow you to read

what's behind the code. It can be a number of things like a business card, an image, a text file to only name a few, but in this case it was a link to a coupon offering a 50% discount on our next visit!

Talk about embracing new technology!

My goal here is not to suggest a specific strategy. My goal in this chapter is to make you realize that although traditional marketing is no longer as efficient as it used to be, it's not dead! In fact if you follow the suggestions I will give you in this chapter your old marketing strategies could actually beat new marketing strategies in terms of ROI! I know that's a big claim but I assure you that once you read this chapter you'll be better off then you were when you started. That's my promise to you.

Is Traditional Marketing dead?

As an internet marketing consultant, when clients hire me they expect me to say traditional marketing is no longer efficient and that nowadays there's nothing better than internet marketing, period. In fact most of the time they often come out saying it themselves!

The truth is that it's exactly what I tell them! But, I immediately clarify this statement by saying: "Traditional marketing, <u>as you know it</u>, is dead"...

You see, traditional marketing "as you know it" is no longer efficient for a number of reasons but instead of boring you with pages of theory, let me ask you this:

When you read the paper and see a short ad that says call 1-800-buy-today or come visit us at 555 Main St., is there the slightest chance you will do either one of these call to action if you're not "really" interested? Didn't think so...

But what about if there was a simple but catchy URL on that ad which was designed to get you curious about something that is not necessarily something that you are "really" interested in but were curious about. Would you check it out on your smart phone or even your computer if it's close by?

What's the difference between the two?

One requires a significant commitment while the other leaves you in your comfort zone which makes it easier for the prospect to "check it out" since it's so unthreatening.

As a merchant, you get to talk to as prospect much longer which gives you more time to sell your products or services to them and you can do so in the format of your choice whether its text or video or both for as long as you want, albeit you still need to be efficient in your approach otherwise they will "X out" fast!

So are you starting to see the big picture here? It doesn't matter if it's an ad in the paper, a TV commercial, a billboard or a radio ad, traditional marketing is NOT dead. It just needs to be combined to, you guessed it, internet marketing.

Traditional Marketing vs. Internet Marketing

Let me make a quick comparison between traditional marketing and internet marketing to drive my point deeper into your psyche:

First off even though traditional marketing can be used very specifically to answer very specific needs, it is most often used in a way called: "interruption marketing". Think of a billboard you see while driving by, a commercial on TV you immediately fast forward since you recorded it in advance, a radio ad interrupting your favorite song... you get the picture.

This kind of marketing has been used for ever and continues to be used simply because it works. In the same fashion as fishing with a 5 mile wide networks these kinds of ads are non-targeted but in the end get customers but the reality is that very few businesses can afford such luxury these days thus it is important, for such businesses n a small marketing budget to be as targeted as possible which is difficult to do with traditional marketing, as you know it.

Internet marketing by contrast allows you to target very specifically. For example: if you type in "red with white stripes women running shoes" in Google you will see ads about this kind of shoes for sure. This means that if you sell this product, ONLY those who enter this keyword phrase will ever see your ad! How targeted is that!
Let's recap:

Traditional marketing

- It's expensive
- Can't be tracked efficiently,

- Need to work a lot to convince people that are not really interested in my products in the first place
- I need to use a wide array of marketing strategies to see significant results which makes it time consuming to manage

Internet marketing

- There are very inexpensive and even free methods available
- I can easily track what works and what doesn't work,
- I can only focus on my ideal clients ie the ones that really need my products
- I can focus on one or two targeted methods and simply work on optimizing them until I get a positive ROI at which point I can just "rinse and repeat"?

At this point we could be tempted to say: Why should I bother with traditional marketing anymore?

If you weren't a local business I'd say you are right since you could probably use the internet to sell your products online but as a local business you need to be aware of the fact that although internet marketing is growing by leaps and bounds your clients are still going to read the papers, listen to the radio, notice the billboards and watch TV, to only name a few methods.

What this means is that you still should embrace traditional marketing, but with a twist.

Traditional marketing with a twist please

OK we've seen so far that traditional marketing is no longer as effective as it once was given the arrival of internet marketing but I also explained that you shouldn't drop your old ways completely. I also mentioned that to be efficient you needed to add internet marketing to it.

We will now look at what I meant by this:

I already addressed the main reasons why traditional marketing was so inefficient but in a nutshell it's simply because it requires a big commitment from your prospects to follow the usual call to actions such strategies require ie call us or visit us.

With internet marketing we can resolve this problem by creating an online platform which can take many forms:

- Website
- Single Web page (sales letter with a call to action)
- Facebook page
- Blog
- Capture page

More and more often, we see newspaper and magazine ads use at least a website URL to offer more information to the readers. So, whether you use a QR code or not, as long as there is a way to get the reader to an online platform where you can continue your "conversation" with them, you've achieved your goal.

So you see, it's not very complicated but as I alluded to earlier, once you get them to go on your web platform you need to be efficient at confirming their attention by confirming, quickly, that you have an answer to their problem(s) by grabbing their attention right away, keeping their attention by increasing their interest to learn more and before asking for the sale you need to stimulate their desire to acquire your products or services.

Yes it means more work, but it's going to be worth it because since you'll be generating a lot more prospects this way the bottom line is that you will be selling more of your products and/or services.

That being said I now want to give you the special recipe to becoming the leader in your field in a matter of weeks!

If you were reading this diagonally, standing up , I suggest you now sit down and pay close attention because this next section will change how you market your product forever! I'm not kidding...

Traditional marketing on steroids

So far we've addressed the fact that traditional marketing had a single goal now (i.e., to bring the prospects to your online platform.) If you do that and pay attention to your message by writing it with the prospects perspective in mind you will be way ahead of the crowd already but what I'll disclose here will basically guarantee your success!

I call it the APS program (Automated Prospecting System). In a nutshell what this system will do for you is automate the process of acquiring prospects which will them contact you to buy from you and al you'll need to do then is close the sale. Yes all you'll need to do is close pre-sold prospects! You will no longer need to spend most of your time trying to convince people they should buy your products or services, THEY will be the ones who want to buy. How cool is that? Let me tell you what this complete system entails.

For this example I'll focus on the cheaper mediums like ads in local papers, brochures you can distribute physically, if that applies to your business, adding a link on your business cards, stationary, etc...

On your ad you'll want to use a spectacular approach to get people's attention and invite them to visit your url.

That url will in fact be what's called a landing page, or a capture page where you will clarify what you offer which in this case needs to be a bribe of some sort that people will attach a high perceived value to. So much so that they will gladly give you their name and email in return for access to this free offer you are making them.

Once they are on your list it means you'll be able to communicate with them as often as you want! Why is it such a big deal? Well, it is a known fact that you need to repeat a message 6-7 times before a client will buy from you... Now do you understand why a single add in the paper didn't cut it?

Now do you understand why this is even better than just sending them to a page where you need to close them right then and there too? Yes it's better than hoping to get a call from a 4 line ad in the paper but still, you are leaving a lot of money on the tale if you don't do what needs to be done to be able to talk to them at least 6-7 times...

With such a system in place you'll be able to focus on building your credibility in your prospects eyes in a non-threatening way and as such when you do ask for the business it will be a lot easier to get a YES.

Conclusion

I hope that by now you realize how powerful traditional marketing can still be if you spice it up with a good sound internet marketing approach focused on building your credibility before trying to sell them a product or a service.

I challenge you to look around you and notice how much more we now see URLs in traditional marketing channels. Since it is becoming more and more "the norm" I urge you to seriously consider using a system such as my APS program to become a sophisticated marketer before your competition does.

The secret of success is to know something nobody else knows.
Aristotle Onassis

ABOUT ERIC

Eric LeRiche is an ex-pharmaceutical representative with an entrepreneur's heart.

All these years (18) in the pharmaceutical industry helped me hone my sales and marketing skills to a point where I decided to specialize in internet marketing and offer my services to local businesses because I felt I could have a bigger impact there vs. working for multi-billion dollar companies where I was treated like a number while earning them millions of dollars of profits per year!

First I met with local entrepreneurs through the chamber of commerce and other similar venues and realized how much people needed my services simply because internet marketing is not something anybody can "just do". For example some of them spent a fortune building a website but didn't know what to do next... I told them that building a website and not marketing it effectively was like a cell phone without service, or a large billboard in the middle of the desert...

I than helped them get visibility and their sales increased

accordingly so I decided to offer my services to others who were in a similar position and it turns out I'm pretty good at it thus I decided to go full time. I created a website

www.WebSalesSpecialist.com and www.ConsultantMarketingInternet.ca

to explain what I do and am now helping local businesses (and even some all over the world) get their fair share of exposure, and sales, online.

Truly gratifying... :-)

Web Sales Specialist
www.WebSalesSpecialist.com
support@WebSalesSpecialist.com

CHAPTER 13
YOU ARE THE LOCAL GURU

By Rebecca Holman

You Are the Local Guru – Six Tools You Can Use To Take What You Know and Increase Your Credibility While Building an Online Empire!

You Know More Than You Think, and You Have the Power to Influence Your Customers as Well as Your Bottom Line!

Introduction

What if I told you that you as a small business owner possess some very important gifts?

You do. You have probably spent years developing your business, and becoming an expert in your industry. There is always more room in the world for experts.

What if I told you, that you have the power to influence your local community just by being willing to share the knowledge that you have gained about your particular industry?

It's true. People want to know. They crave to learn and to build relationships with people that they trust. Regardless of the industry that you're in, what better person to educate them, teach them, and to be trusted by them, than you.

We live in an interesting age. Technology is advancing at such a rapid pace, and unlike never before people are so willing to engage. They engage with other people, their friends, and increasingly they seek to engage with business owners in their local communities.

This is unprecedented from a marketing standpoint, but also in terms of the fact that it's never been easier for local businesses to gain maximum exposure just by being visible in places where potential customers are looking.

The advent of the Internet, Facebook, Twitter, YouTube and other places has revolutionized the way people interact, and further the way they expect to interact. This means, bluntly, that the old way of doing things is dead.

But, the new age of business marketing is even more exciting. In this report, I'm going to talk to you about six different ways that you can leverage your knowledge as a small business owner.

I'm also going to talk to you about how you can do so in such a way that you can simultaneously influence your local community and add more money to your bottom line with the help of the Internet.

The Tools You Need To Be Using and Why They Will Change Your Business

Every tool that I discuss is important and has the potential to dramatically increase the power of your branding as well as the amount in your bank account each month.

Each one will be accompanied by a short description, how things used to be, what's changed, and what you need to be doing to bring yourself more success.

Laid out like this you'll get the entire picture, and hopefully by the end you'll have some pretty important food for thought.

Tool Number 1: Branded DVD Creation

What It Is

A recording of you doing something, branded with your company information, which customers receive.

Historically

In the days when "portable" media was limited to laser disc, VHS, or the very early days of DVDs it would have been unheard of for companies to produce branded content to distribute to the masses, or even in small batches unless they had a large marketing budget. People however, are visually oriented and have always responded well to advertising cues this way.

Today With a Twist

Today, things have changed. We've moved from VHS to DVD. From the DVD to the High Definition Blu-Ray, and from those forms of portable media to hand held devices that contain more computer power than many of the first and second generation space fleet.

People still love videos. In fact, using video to market your business is a great method. Consumers are just as likely to watch them online, or as a download as they are to watch something on a disk. In fact, many consumers are more likely to watch streaming videos in most cases but there are exceptions.

Training video series where instruction is taking place is one of these exceptions. Also, it is incredibly easy, and very inexpensive to have your video content turned into small or large scale mass produced and branded DVD's that you don't even have to keep on hand.

Imagine giving a talk or a series of talks locally. Now imagine how much greater your reach could be if you could have that talk filmed and put onto a DVD which could then be dispatched out to any customer either for free or for a fee. How much do you think this would add to your bottom line, either directly or indirectly?

What You Should Do

Think about what you could show on video, what do your customers want to know about?

Tool Number 2: Digital Product Creation

What It Is

Taking your knowledge and putting it into digital form so people can purchase or benefit from it.

Historically

Digital product creation didn't really exist until the internet came along, and even still it wasn't that widely used until the internet became such a strong force in people's homes.

Are you aware that, even in the toughest economy when it seems like no one is buying, that people will still buy online? It's true, whether it's through an online retailer, or maybe they're investing in a digital information product that they hope will give them some new knowledge or a new skillset that will change their situation.

Today With a Twist

Digital product creation is so innovative today because of that very fact, people will invest in interesting things they see on the internet, which they feel might help them learn something, or change their current situation.

Many digital products are priced in such a way that there is a low barrier to entry in the first place, and to the consumer this just makes sense, especially if it's something they want to learn.

As a business owner, you are already an expert in your industry. There is no reason not to take some of that knowledge you have, and expand your brand out to include digital product offerings on top of whatever else you sell.

This is the case regardless of the industry you are in. A digital product can be a streaming video course, a paid series of downloadable lectures, an e-book, or any combination of the above. Even at low prices, this kind of thing can add a lot of money to your bank account especially if you sell other things along with the digital products, or sell other things to the people who bought your digital products.

What You Should Do

Think about how you can transform your knowledge into a digital product, and what else you can market to your consumers over the course of following up with them.

Tool Number 3: Self-Publishing to Become an Author

What It Is

Publishing and marketing your own book to widen your influence and give yourself instant credibility.

Historically

Say the word "published author" at any event in the not too recent past and most people's eyes glazed over at the very thought of how much work that must have been to get a book deal, and how lucky that certain person must have been.

That's because, before self-publishing came into its own, that type of occurrence was just about the only way to be considered a published author, or at least a respectable published author.

Today With a Twist

Today however, the tides have turned. Amazon's CreateSpace™ and other self-publishing services like LuLu® have gained respect, streamlined the process and made it very easy for business owners, and others with such a desire to publish their own books.

Distribution deals are also in place such that with the proper marketing it's possible to get into bookstores, be sold on Amazon.com and even end up a New York Times Best Seller. The best part about it all? It's all print-on-demand so you don't even have to stock large quantities of your own book, as the case used to be.

Being that it's so easy to become a published author these days, and relatively easy to become a popular one if some basic marketing principles are observed, it's not hard to realize that writing a book is the best way to gain instant credibility.

This works also for digital e-books that we discussed previously, but a physical book goes a long way in certain circles in terms of expanding your sphere of influence, and the costs and trouble overall are quite minimal especially considering what it could do for your business if you sold the books, or if you gave them as a free bonus or distributed them to other high powered individuals in your local area or within your industry. You = instant expert.

What You Should Do

Think about what topic you would write your book on, and look into a self-publishing service like CreateSpace™.

Tool Number 4: Digital Publishing to Increase Your Exposure

What It Is

Taking your book or other content and making it accessible for e-book readers.

Historically

This is another tool that's excellent for business owners which really doesn't have that much history just because it's only been fairly recently that e-book readers have become popular, and led to an increased need for content that could be viewed on them.

Today With a Twist

Since e-book readers have become incredibly popular however, especially the Amazon Kindle, the demand for a library of content specifically for e-book readers is booming.

E-books and digital books for e-book platforms like this are quickly outpacing physical books in sales, and much like people generally have a preference for purchasing online, a good number of people prefer this kind of "book" experience over a physical book.

There are many reasons for this, but low barrier to entry (digital books cost less than physical books,) convenience (these kinds of books can be delivered wirelessly meaning no shipping costs or wait time) and space saving benefits are among the primary reasons for this preference.

Many books can be carried on a device that is the size of a single book, which is very appealing for booklovers who do not want to haul their entire physical library around with them everywhere but have no problem carrying another productivity device.

If you've written a physical book, or created a digital product of any kind, it makes sense to convert the content into a format that can be easily accessible via ebook reader. This is something else you can sell or promote to expand your company brand recognition, and to build a loyal following.

What You Should Do

Look into how a book or product is converted to be compatible with and downloadable on the Kindle marketplace, and determine several ways this type of digital publishing could be used in your marketing.

Tool Number 5: Public Speaking Skills for Presentations and Workshop

What It Is

Conquering your fear of public speaking to share your unique knowledge.

Historically

Public speaking and giving seminars in person is one of the few tools mentioned where technology has not played as much a role in innovation (a discussion on how that's actually occurred is coming up next) in that the way things used to be, for the most part are still the same today.

The fact of the matter is, the more face time you have as a business owner with your potential customers, other people in your industry and those in competing industries who could bring you business, the greater your chances of, well, getting business from them.

People buy from those they know, like and trust, and if people can see you or hear you and you're teaching them something or solving a problem, then you instantly own a piece of their consumer heart.

Public speaking is historically known as one of the biggest fears we face as a species, but to overcome this, now or in the past has had amazing results.

Today With a Twist

All of the above is still true today. However, because consumers are more aware of opportunities and more likely to want to engage with the businesses they are invested in, curious about or which were previously unknown to them there are more opportunities than ever to teach people, to give presentations, to speak in front of influential individuals and generally to get yourself and your business out there in front of people.

You don't have to be the best public speaker at first, there are classes along with local Toastmasters groups that you can attend to deal with your fear, and the more you do it, the better you will become.

Not only is public speaking one of the highest paid professions out there, and one which often comes with endorsement deals of its own, it is also very possible to sell items at conferences and speaking engagements, or to make money off of referrals that you get because of your participation, and people's interest in your business.

Yet, this tool is often overlooked by many business owners. Don't under estimate your abilities.

What You Should Do

Determine what you might speak about if you had to do an impromptu presentation for a room of 25-50 people. Also look into a Toastmasters group if your nerves get the best of you.

Tool Number 6: Conducting a Webinar

What It Is

A webinar is like a seminar, except it is conducted online, and can reach more people.

Historically

As we've said with several of the other tools, the past was limiting in many ways even if it didn't mean to be, just because the technology didn't exist for business owners to expand beyond their local area without considerable effort.

This was acceptable, and expected, and from that acceptance came the "Mom and Pop" local brands that were so prevalent before the advent of big box stores. Even the business owners who did get out on the seminar or trade show were limited by how far they could drive, how often they wanted to fly, or how many engagements they could do in a week or in a year.

Today With a Twist

With the help of the internet and a 3rd party software client like Go2Webinar, a seminar becomes a webinar and those previously discussed limitations are no longer valid.

It is possible to give one presentation that has thousands of attendees from all over the world. They are all interested in your product or service and what you have to say, and a good percentage of them will buy whatever it is that you sell at the end of your webinar should you choose to offer them something (and you should.)

You could have a series of webinars, each covering a different topic every day for a certain number of days, every week or every month also for a set period, engage with your customers, and make money all without having to leave your house.

Similarly, the webinar process is also able to be automated, which means you record a webinar, or a webinar series, and then they are available for people to "attend" or listen to on a continuous basis if setup correctly. This means you could go through the process once and then with a few tweaks so as to not be deceitful, have your webinars running almost completely on autopilot making you money and generating leads for you without you having to constantly be present.

What You Should Do

Look into a service like Go2Webinar and become proficient with PowerPoint for your webinar presentations after determining your topic.

In conclusion, we have outlined just a few ways that you take what you have learned in your career and leverage it to create a new and possibly fulfilling side income. By offering your knowledge you are passing on your skills to more people that you would reach just in the context of your business office or storefront alone. You have spent years accumulating what you know, why not share it with the many people that would benefit from your years of hard work and learning?

The 21st century offers anyone that would like to, a chance to be a guru, how about you?

CHAPTER 14

21st CENTURY MARKETING SECRETS FOR SMALL BUSINESS OWNERS

By Rebecca Holman

Introduction

As a small business owner, you probably agree that your most important asset is your customers, right? Here's the thing though, it's not just about your customers.

It's about the relationship you build with them and what you do with them once you have them, that makes you money at the end of the day.

If you've never thought about it like that before, repeat that last line to yourself. It's not just about your customers, but the relationship that you build with them and what you do with them once you have them.

Getting new customers and building lasting relationships with those that you served in the past is easier than ever. This is especially true given the fact that technology abounds in the 21st century, and more than that, it's advancing at a rapid pace.

Technology is exciting, and whether they feel totally comfortable with it or not, people are so much more likely to use that technology than they ever have been in the past.

In this chapter, I'm going to share with you six 21st century marketing secrets that you as a small business owner should be taking full advantage of.

Beyond that, I'm going to detail in-depth about why it's so important to be on top of your game no matter which industry you're in, otherwise you're missing out big time.

The Secrets, Their Pasts, and Their Current Truths

As mentioned, I will reveal some secrets few small business owners know. Each secret will be accompanied by a real-world application, what the truth used to be, what the truth is now, and what you need to be doing to bring yourself into the new era.

This way, you will have the entire picture, and hopefully by the end you will have some points to take action on.

Secret Number 1: If You Have a Website, Chances Are, It's Not Serving You

Translation

There's more to a great website than a slick design.

The Old Way

In the old days, when the internet was new, way back in the 1990s, and before the concept of something "going viral" was a pop culture phenomenon, designing websites was a different animal than it is today. Web design companies usually consisted of two types:

1. Those that built simple, but not always aesthetically pleasing, websites and made their money on the basis of giving a business a "presence" on the web in its infancy.

or

2. Those that built flashy sites which were pretty and engaging at first glance, but which usually ended up being poorly laid out and not functional for anyone needing any kind of information.

Neither of these situations was ideal, unless you were a web designer, of course.

Along this same vein, large companies sprung up offering "easy to build templates" or website packages where business owners could have their whole operation up and running within a matter of hours.

What they don't say however, is that each site pretty much looks the same, and since they own the template and other important aspects, if a business owner cancels at any time, or violates their usage contract somehow, then the site is instantly taken down. In a case like this, the business owner has no control of the things which they do not own.

The New Reality

While it's still somewhat common to see instances of what's mentioned above, having a web presence that is functional and built on a platform that is easy to use is of primary importance. Your website doesn't have to be flashy in order to get the job done. In fact, "flashy" can actually drive customers away.

Search engines are also much more intelligent and robust than they were when the internet began. This means that having a website that is search engine optimized, and easy to update is more important than ever.

Whether you manage it yourself, or have someone else do it, your website, at a bare minimum should:

- Be branded with your company logo. You want people to come to recognize your product.

- Be easy on the eyes, but not overly done. You want to minimize distractions so your customers have limited options, can clearly see your call to action and are not overwhelmed.

- Be designed so that your contact information is among the first things visible on the page. You don't want to make it difficult for people to find what they're after, and in 99% of cases, it's your contact information.

What You Need To Be Doing

Examine your website, and/or current hosting situation to ensure that you have at least some degree of control. Have clear calls to action on your front page near the top of your website, not hidden down near the bottom.

Secret Number 2: Most Advertising Costs More Than It's Worth

Translation

Most of your advertising money is being wasted these days!

The Old Way

Before technology became such an integral part of our lives, our methods of communication were pretty limited, which in turn meant that advertising methods for business were pretty limited as well.

Cold calling, direct mail, newspaper classified ads, phone book advertising, and hoping that customers would pass along a good word to their friends were pretty much it, and they were all expensive.

For bigger businesses, local TV or radio ads may have also been an option but even their scope was limited inherently by the fact that they could never really reach outside of a business's surrounding area.

Businesses used these methods and squeaked by though justifying the cost because they either had to go this route or die.

The New Reality

Things have changed dramatically. Over 90% of consumers have turned to their smartphones, their streaming video infused, high speed internet connection, and they've also turned to their social media profiles.

They have turned to technology over phone books, newspaper classifieds and with the invention of television viewing on demand better known as TIVO, most people do not even acknowledge television ads in the same way that they used to.

In fact, these days, one of the first places that a potential customer of yours, no matter which industry you're in, is likely to go when trying to find out more information about your business, is the internet. This means frankly, if you don't have a presence on the internet, or if your business is negatively represented on the internet, you're setting yourself up for failure.

What You Need To Be Doing

Expand your thinking, and move away from costly advertising, particularly print ads, which are producing almost no ROI. It's not where people are looking.

Secret Number 3: Email Lists & Partnerships Can Be Easy Money

Translation

You need to be contacting past and future prospects and establishing relationships with businesses complementary to yours.

The Old Way

As with secret number 2 above, in the past it was either very difficult or potentially very time consuming to build lucrative partnerships between two businesses no matter how complementary their products or services might have been to a particular pool of customers.

Without technology to expedite the process, and open the lines of communication, business owners were limited to

- Direct marketing and post card drops.
- Cold calling, door hangers, trade shows and fairs

The New Reality

Today the modern small business owner has unlimited and automated ways to reach their customers, email marketing has been a major boon to businesses worldwide.

The Internet has offered small businesses a chance to play with the big boys. With little capital investment, you can gather information about your core customer base and market directly to their needs and demographics.

Also many businesses have found that Joint Venturing can spread their dollars even further. A Real Estate Agent that focuses on high end real estate can work in conjunction with an outfitter that caters to the very people that want to make the move to their favorite vacation spot.

What You Need To Be Doing

Review ways to incorporate how to use email marketing to connect with, and therefore potentially make more money from, current customers as well as attracting new ones.

Secret Number 4: Smartphone Usage Is Pervasive and Your Biz Can Benefit

Translation

A website optimized for people on mobile phones, and text message marketing will put you ahead of the pack.

The Old Way

Prior to cell phones being so commonly used by all levels of society, the business owner had to reach out to their clients via expensive mediums such as expensive Yellow Page ads and paper advertising. Costs were high, returns were low and growing lower as more people turned to digital mediums.

The New Reality

Currently you can gain access to low cost Keyword Texting campaigns called "SMS" texting.

The average email sits for a day or more or is not even read, while a text message is looked at almost immediately. So, the first businesses to embrace this medium will be able to capitalize on this new and exploding marketing technique.

As more of your customers move to "Smart" phones, they will be searching for you on their cell phones, which have small screens. As cell phones are now surpassing computers in sales, it is important that your site have not just an online presence but one that allows your site to be user friendly on mobile phones and tablets.

The majority of people that are searching on their phones are seeking basic information. Where are you located, how to contact you and maybe to see if you have any coupons specials. Modern texting programs make this both inexpensive to implement as well as make you accessible to the very people that are currently searching for you.

What You Need To Be Doing

All small business owners need to be researching this new and very dynamic method of finding and retaining their customers. Engagement at this top of mind awareness level has never before been so easy and so inexpensive to implement.

Secret Number 5: Publicity Isn't Just For Celebrities

Translation

Videos, a blog and press releases will maximize your exposure.

The Old Way

Prior to 2005, it was expensive and daunting for a small business owner to consider creating a TV ad for their business. Professional writers, videographers, camera people and actors needed to be hired and scripts written. For a local small business hardware store to compete with Sears would have been impossible.

The New Reality

In 2005, YouTube was born and video technology has never been the same. It is now easy and very inexpensive to have a professionally created video on the Internet in a matter of hours, not days or weeks.

Now with the cost of a camera under $200, videos can be created and uploaded to the Internet. Using video and images on your website or in Press Releases and other advertising has proven to increase conversion rates significantly.

What You Need To Be Doing

You can update your blog, Facebook status, and upload a video from virtually any place on the planet. Your ability to interface and communicate with your customers is really at the end of your hand in your cell phone.

Secret Number 6: Social Media Is Not a Fad

Translation

You need a Facebook Page for your business, and it won't hurt you to be "Social."

The Old Way

When Google was young and the Dot Com bubble was bursting, many people said that the Internet could never last. Now with over 700 million users on Facebook alone and untold billions of sales being made every year, it looks like the naysayers were very, very wrong.

In rural America small towns, word of mouth may still work. You know your customers personally and you go to BBQs at their homes and tailgate at the local football game. Once a town grows to over 100,000 and beyond, it becomes very challenging to know your customers personally and with new people coming and going so quickly in this transient world, it is more and more challenging to depend on the old fashioned belly to belly, hand shake and word of mouth referral system.

The New Reality

Considering that even rice paddy farmers in the wilds of Vietnam use cell phone technology to sell their crops, it behooves the typical western business owner to get with the social program.

Your customers are being increasingly attached to their technology toys. Smart cell phones, iPads, and Netbooks make it so easy for people to take their Internet engagement everywhere. No longer are they looking you up in the Yellow pages, they are letting their fingers do the walking across their keyboards to find you.

As I mentioned above, there are over 700 million people on Facebook. In aggregate, people are on Facebook for a total of over 700 billion minutes a month according to DigitalBuzz.com. 48% of 18-34 year olds check Facebook as soon as they wake up. 72% of all US Internet users are now on Facebook. So, do you see the trend here, and why you need to be where your customers are?

What You Need To Be Doing

It is really easy to get a presence on the Internet. By seeking out a competent Internet Marketing professional you can have access to many touch points to reach out to your customer base. Now it has never been so easy to engage and at the same time so complicated. You deserve to have a portion of this traffic finding you, the choice is yours.

What This Means for You as a Business Owner

As you can see from just a few of the secrets that we have revealed above, the small business owner can thrive in this new market environment. Many of these secrets have a low cost to entry and can have impressive results in a short period of time.

Gone are the days of expensive Yellow Page ads or newspaper ads that are read one day and are in the bottom of the bird cage the next. Now you, the small business owner, can play with the likes of Sears and WalMart. With a small fraction of their marketing budget you can still touch thousands of potential clients at the click of a button.

What is the important take away here is that the Internet is here to stay, and mobile marketing and social media engagement is hot on the horizon for the next wave of potential exposure to new customers. Will you be there? Will you be found?

These topics, while somewhat simple to understand still do take some experience to know how to finesse them to extract their highest potential and the most bang for your buck. It is the recommendation of this author to explore the options that a professional Internet Marketer can bring to your bottom line.

If you want more customers ringing your phone then push for professional assistance because these marketing concepts need to be executed correctly over time and as a small business owner it is worth your time to invest in someone that can do it correctly. This is a changing landscape and it is the job of a Professional Internet Marketer to keep abreast of those changes.

ABOUT REBECCA

Rebecca Holman has created, developed and optimized over 100 sites during the last 2 years. She has been working within the Internet marketing space since 1999 working for Software startup companies taking them to the point of being successfully purchased by Fortune 500 companies.

Her Search Engine Marketing and Search Engine Optimization experience is an outgrowth of those many years of working on the Internet since its early days. Google changes its algorithms about 140+ times a year...as a professional Rebecca credits her success with keeping up on that information for her many satisfied clients... helping to keep them ahead of their competition.

Originally from Queens, NY, Rebecca has lived in Montana for over 25 years and graduated with honors from the University of Montana. She enjoys the outdoors with her black lab and close friends, hiking, biking and kayaking in the area surrounding her home in Montana.

Please connect with Rebecca Holman on her LinkedIn page http://www.linkedin.com/in/seodivarebeccaholman

CHAPTER 15

FIVE WAYS TO ATTRACT NEW CUSTOMERS AND INCREASE SALES USING THE INTERNET

By Robert Stanley

1—Viral marketing with Social Media

Viral marketing is effective and attractive. Although it is only effective when properly architected to spread as expected, it is still attractive because it is essentially an automated referral system that requires no work once you have started it. And it is no secret that for small businesses, referrals are one of the best sources of new customers. So, the question is...

How do you use social media to create viral sales and new customers?

First, you need an offer or idea that has the potential to

spread by word of mouth (go viral), and second, you need a network or platform that makes the process of sharing the offer or idea very easy.

Let's discuss the offer. In my opinion, the offer needs to be architected in a way that does more than simply generate brand awareness. It needs to bring the possibility of new purchases and appointments. Ideally, your offer should have three elements in order to be successful:

1. It must be extremely compelling—$19 Oil Change

2. It must have a *group* or *social* element—$9 Oil Change (refer two friends) Free (refer four friends)

3. A Profitable Add-on—lube, tune-up, filters, wipers, brakes, etc.

In this example, the oil change is designed to get customers in the door. The group offer is designed to create a viral effect by inviting two or four more friends.

Before the days of Social Media, this would require a fair amount of paper-tracking. Tracking should still be done, but with sites like Facebook, this could be an automated and instantly viral campaign. We will put the technical details aside for now. All you need to know is that coupons and offers shared on Facebook can reach hundreds, even thousands, of your target customers in only a few minutes. And the best part is that it would be entirely referral-based—warm prospects sent by friends.

Of course, quality services and products must be delivered in this scenario or you might end up with a viral tongue-lashing. But let's assume you are offering only the very best of the best. This still begs the question...

How Might You Profit From This Viral Campaign?

Good question. Probably the most overlooked element of any offer, viral or otherwise, is the need for profitable add-ons or upgrades. In this example, it is unlikely that a business could sustain itself financially selling $9–$19 oil changes. The labor costs alone would kill the profits, and maybe even the business.

The key to success when presenting low-priced offers is to carefully select and suggest add-on and premium-purchase options to the customer. Many restaurants do this daily with super-sized drinks and *à la carte* soups or salads. My own testing suggests that between twenty and thirty percent, or even more, will say yes to whatever you may be offering as a premium add-on. And in the automotive business, it could be a pretty large payout, with bigger ticket repairs or advanced maintenance.

Summary

Viral marketing became a reality with the powerful addition of social media and a compelling offer. Be sure to carefully select both your offer and premium add-ons to maximize your profits. Viral marketing alone cannot sustain your business, but it can be a welcome boost when a successful campaign is launched.

2—Paid Advertising Online

Paid advertising can bring instant profits. However, just like our viral offers, we will need some compelling offers and add-ons to make it work. First, let's start with the basics and explain what it is, and how to use it.

What is Online Advertising?

There are essentially two major forms; paid-search and

content-based advertising. Paid-search or search engine marketing (SEM) is simply purchased placement within the search engine results. So when a consumer searches for "local auto repair shops", your website will appear.

This form of advertising is extremely powerful when combined as a problem, solution, match. Example: Search phrase = " New Tire Prices"; Advertisement = "Looking for Tires?". When the consumer clicks on the advertisement, you have to keep them interested by having that compelling offer in place. And once they come into the store, you have your valuable add-ons ready for presentation.

Content-based advertising is worth mentioning, but is probably not one you should start with. It essentially involves images, banners and other website-based advertising. You can do this on almost any website, including Facebook and LinkedIn.

The downside to content-based advertising is that the people seeing your ads aren't necessarily looking for what you have to offer. So, it is a numbers game, which if done incorrectly, can easily cost you hundreds of dollars with nothing to show for it.

However, Facebook in particular is interesting because you have the ability to combine paid advertising with viral marketing. This provides an opportunity to place your viral offer in front of thousands of people in less than twenty-four hours. Where else can you go, where you can instantly attract customers and referrals without leaving your office?

The easiest way to find out what your competitors are doing online is to simply go to Google.com and search as if you were a customer. Then look for obvious competitors in the paid-search results, and spy on their offers and websites. If you can, you might want to actually purchase something, and spy on the entire process.

Summary

Online advertising puts your products and services in front of prospects in need. You can see immediate results with paid advertising, given the proper structure and offers. With online advertising, it is possible to see fast results, which makes it an excellent platform to test new offers, or even launch a product or service.

3—Online Coupon Systems

Have you heard of Groupon? At this moment, it is a very popular and very effective form of marketing. It is the modern-day Val-Pack printed coupon system turned Internet coupon system.

In case you're not aware of Groupon, it is an Internet-based, local coupon system designed to drive new customers to local businesses. This is done primarily by using extreme discounts of at least fifty percent off retail pricing. In order to place a coupon advertisement on their site, you MUST have a compelling offer which is either approved or denied, based on how well it may perform.

Coupon seekers actually have to prepay in order to get the deal you're offering. Many claim that a fair percentage of the purchasers never actually use the coupon, despite having paid for it. This varies depending upon the price and offer type, but unclaimed coupons are seen as high as twenty percent So, if you set your offer limit to 100 units, at a price of $19, you could end up with an extra $200 from the advertisement.

Once the advertisement is "live", it may or may not actually work. If the response to your coupon offer is too low, then the coupon will be pulled, and purchasers will be refunded.

So it may take some trial and error to produce one that works for your business. Be sure to keep season changes and holidays in mind as you craft your offer.

Groupon maintains a huge database of coupon seekers, in all major cities, which is how they manage to drive so much business. Once you have your discount offer ready and approved, they feature it using their website and email lists. They also have a mobile Web application that automatically notifies customers of new deals.

Common Coupon Dangers

Despite their recent popularity, online coupon systems also have some pitfalls; the sudden unplanned rush of customers from sites like Groupon can hurt your business. Failure to deliver on your promised goods and services can hurt your reputation, and too many discounted sales can kill your profit.

There is another hidden danger with this method of marketing—the customer. In many cases, deep discounts attract "discount seekers", which means that the expectation of creating return business may be a dream. As soon as the discount is gone, the discount seeker is gone.

Protecting Your Profits

Here are a few simple things you can do to counter the downside risks. These simple suggestions will prepare you for the mad rush, and help you profit despite the costly discounts:

1. Discount Registration—force all those who submit a coupon to also register for future discount offers. This will allow you to follow-up and offer other specials without having to deal with Groupon. To do this you will need to keep a customer database. IMPORTANT NOTE: This is why Groupon is so powerful because they have the customer database.

2. Premium Upgrades—all your discount offers should include premium upgrades. As many as twenty to thirty percent of the discount buyers will take upgrade options when offered. So, if you were offering pedicures for $15, offer a deluxe manicure upgrade for $25. Premium goods and services can cover the costs or losses of all the discounts provided by the initial offer. This also has the added benefit of immediately separating the discount seeker form the quality, long-term customer.

3. Follow-up Offers—before your discount ever hits the street, you should have identified upgrade offers and follow-up offers for your discount seeker list. This is the reason you need to create a registration list. A thirty-day follow-up campaign can take your discount offer from loss to profit in short order. In addition to the premium upgrade, this also allows you to identify more long-term customers.

Summary

Coupons can provide you with a quick influx of new customers when you craft the proper offer. It is important to recognize that most coupon shoppers are not repeat customers, which means you will have to quickly sort your ideal customers from the price-frenzied mob. Without coupon marketing, you may be missing out on new ways to drive more customers and business; but be sure to have your premium offers and follow-up systems in place in order to maximize your profit.

4—Email Newsletters

Have you seen the commercials? Constant-Contact is probably the most active email subscription and newsletter provider in the market. They actively target small businesses and promote the power of email marketing via newsletters.

Does Email Marketing Work?

Yes and No. Like many forms of marketing, HOW it is used impacts its effectiveness. I often hear business owners saying things like, "I never read my email, it is all junk...", but that is a gross generalization. Do they read email from their wife, friend, father, mother or brother?... of course! If they are a fishing enthusiast, and receive monthly updates on the latest techniques, hot locations, fishing vacations or new products, do they read those emails?... absolutely!

Here are a few elements that will help improve your email marketing efforts:

1. Permission—the person receiving your email must have asked to receive information and updates from you. Buying lists of random email, sand-blasting out your offer, is not only illegal, but also ineffective. So, make sure you are communicating with people who want to hear from you.

2. Regularity—sending email only once a month will likely do more harm than good. Unfortunately, the squeaky wheel will get the grease, and if you only squeak once a month, you will rarely be heard. DO NOT be afraid of "making them angry". If your email subscribers don't like what you're sending, you don't want them on your list anyway. Ideally, you should communicate daily for the first week that someone is added to your list, and then weekly to maintain your communication channel.

3. Relevance—if someone subscribes to your email list or newsletter try to remain relevant. Current news, trends and education-based selling is your best bet. This ties back to regularity because if you only email your information once a quarter then you probably won't be seen as relevant. Daily news exists because information and events change daily. Stay relevant and maintain a frequent and consistent interval.

4. Entertainment—even the most boring topics can gain readership if they contain elements of entertainment. That's the reason the daily paper has crosswords and cartoons. Everyone needs a break from the day-to-day news and work-related information. Be sure to add some stories, comics or jokes to keep your readers

interested.

Using Email Newsletters

Newsletters are an excellent, non-offensive form of email marketing that help to keep an open line of communication with your clients and prospects.

Why is that important?

Newsletters provide your business with a marketing communication channel that sounds more like news rather than a blatant sales pitch. It keeps your company brand in front of the customer and "in-mind" when it is time to buy. If your business is seasonal, then it is critical; it maintains the relationship despite the lack of active purchases.

And more importantly, when it is time to "sell", you can send out an email offer between newsletter releases. You email can say something like "Special offer for newsletter subscribers," or "Member-only special for October." Emails like this are more effective when you warn of an upcoming special in the newsletter because you can refer back to the newsletter in your email offer. This is referred to as "reason why copy," and has strong physiological benefits. Anytime you can justify your actions with reasons, they are more likely to be accepted.

Other Newsletter Benefits

Event marketing–if you hold regular events, either virtual or in-person, you probably want to have good attendance. Nothing is worse than holding an event, only to have two or three people show up.

Maintaining a newsletter allows you the opportunity to broadcast your event to your customers and vendors. This creates a certain amount of insurance for any business event that you hold. It works well for trade-shows, online seminars (webinars), training events, wine dinners, open houses, and more.

Summary

Newsletters can help you build your brand, communicate your events, and connect with your clients on a more personal level. Without newsletter marketing, your voice, value and company message will be left to your infrequent personal contact, or your sales and support staff, who may not be as effective at communicating your company messages as the company leaders.

5—Online Seminars and Training

Education-based selling is more effective and efficient than ever before. And you do not have attend a tradeshow or rent a booth to reach your prospects. With modern advances in web video and education platforms, it is inexpensive and relatively easy to do virtually.

Just look at online universities, as an example. Despite the arguments related to quality or viability, these educational institutions have created a new norm. More and more people are using Internet-based systems to educate themselves both formally and informally. This new acceptance of online education opens the door for you to reach prospects in new ways.

Anyone with a high-speed Internet connection is within your reach. And, due to the global reach of the World Wide Web, you can sell outside the realm of your local market. This is GREAT NEWS because you can side-step issues with the local economy, while still maintaining a local and global business presence. Below are two proven Internet-based training methods you can use to get more clients through education-based selling.

Webinars/Online Seminars—online events such as webinars and seminars offer a "virtual sales meeting" and dedicated face-time with your prospects. Imagine having thirty minutes to an hour to sell your company or your services to executives and decision makers without leaving your office. More importantly, imagine presenting to tens, hundreds, or even thousands of prospects all at once. No more drive times, cancelled appointments or delayed flights; just pure, efficient selling.

Online Training—online training can be anything from a simple eBook to a complete online education system. You can either sell your training as the do-it-yourself (DIY) solution, or give it away to demonstrate your knowledge and the value of a done-for-you service. For example, an auto mechanic could have a video series on car maintenance that shows all the tools needed, the issues to avoid, and more. Most DIY beginners fail to estimate the time, tools and training needed to properly perform tasks that a professional can provide.

Look around. Pay careful attention to what the major players and industry associations are doing online. You may notice that they are doing more event-driven marketing; webinars, videos, and live events with video streaming over the Internet, are all methods currently being used successfully all over the world.

In particular, take a careful look at trade organizations and certification institutes. They have mastered the art of education-based selling with teaser content, white papers and online seminars. This type of online and event-driven marketing provides three primary benefits that can accelerate the sales process for your company:

Credibility—when taking the role of instructor or authority, you are granted a certain level of credibility without the need for client references, case studies or price comparisons. We are trained from an early age that the "teacher" is the authority; the one that grades our level of understanding. When you teach, you put yourself in a position of authority and instant credibility. This results in less haggling, price shopping and deep questioning. Ultimately, it accelerates the sales and decision-making process.

Trust—when you share knowledge present credibility, it builds a certain level of immediate trust. Trust is THE most important aspect of business relationships and sales. The entire world of selling revolves around this hidden force behind your prospects' buying decision. We trust our teachers, our parents, authors and speakers. They are wise and knowledgeable, and also offer the leadership in areas where we feel weak. Take the leadership position as a teacher, and you will gain the trust of your prospects faster, and with less effort.

Understanding—as you teach, you also gain a deeper understanding of what your prospects want, need and fear. This allows you to address those needs and fears, and eliminate doubts. When blindly selling goods and services, you rarely receive the opportunity to interact with customers. This results in limited understanding of what your prospects really want. A lack of understanding can lead to unexplained lost sales and profits. Teaching and presenting allows you to step into your prospects shoes through a series of interactions. This is the ultimate form of business intelligence, and it will give you a significant advantage over the competition.

Summary

Online training can position you and your company as a leader in your industry. The process of teaching builds instant credibility and trust, together with a deeper understanding of your market. It is inexpensive when compared to traditional door-to-door selling, and creates an environment where selling many-to-one is a reality. Use this method to accelerate your sales life-cycle and grow your business in record time.

ABOUT ROBERT

Robert Stanley is a marketing consultant, speaker, information marketer and trusted advisor to companies throughout the United States, Canada, UK and Australia.

Expertise Includes:

Local business marketing, list management and email marketing product creation and product launch, SEO and PPC.

You can find more info at http://robertmstanley.com

CHAPTER 16
THE PERFECT STORM FOR VIDEO

By Brian Lee

There's been a lot of buzz about video lately—and for good reason. Technological advances in video production tools and delivery methods have finally made this powerful medium accessible to the masses.

Twenty years ago, you needed a professional studio with expensive cameras, lights, and crew to capture anything on video—and that was just the beginning. You then needed a post-production editing crew to sift through rolls and rolls of film, physically splice them together, and actually ship them off to the TV station or big screen.

Video is at Our Fingertips

Times have changed quite a bit in the last twenty years. Personal video cameras that recorded on film became available in the 70s. The Camcorder allowed the home producer to put video on cassette tape in the 80s. Digital cameras became popular in the 90s; and video started merging with the internet in the 2000s.

It wasn't until the 2010s that cameras became affordable enough, and more importantly, internet *bandwidth became fast enough* to support the video revolution. Mix that with the rise of social media and mobile devices and you have "The Perfect Storm": affordable video production mixed with the ability to reach a massive appetite for video through social media and mobile on the high-bandwidth internet.

Today, you can simply point your mobile phone or pocket video camera and have the video broadcast across the internet in a matter of minutes.

Video Doesn't Have to Be Scary

Even though the power of video is within reach to just about everyone, it still seems daunting to most. It did for me when I was getting my start as a producer in Hollywood; but I quickly learned from my experience at major television networks and reality shows that video wasn't as scary as I initially thought.

Armed with a few simple techniques outlined in the following pages, and some inexpensive video equipment, you can be on your way to communicating with your customers and fans with the most exciting medium available today.

The Perfect Medium

Of all the communication mediums used over the internet, including the written word, audio, still photography, and graphics, video is far and away the most effective for the marketer. Video puts your marketing message in front of your prospects just like a real salesperson.

Video Warms Your Leads

Today's sophisticated marketer realizes that customers want to do business with people they feel comfortable with, not faceless companies. You can't just put up a website or a storefront and expect people to want to buy your products. Building a comfort level with your prospects takes time and energy.

For example, a good salesperson needs seven "touches" with a prospect until they are ready to buy. A touch might be a phone call, a lunch, an email, a postcard, etc. Before the internet, a salesperson had to perform all of these touches with one prospect at a time until they became customers

Today, we can leverage the power of technology to send cold leads a series of automated video blogs, emails, and free trainings that serve as touches so that your prospects are "warm" by the time they call your office. The net effect is less time spent by your sales force and more time closing deals.

Video Conveys Your Personality

Many small businesses make the mistake of creating a faceless brand for their company instead of emphasizing personalities. Remember that customers want to do business with people, not businesses; so it is important to let your prospects get to know your personality, and others with whom they will be interacting.

Video is perfect for this purpose because it allows the viewer to get to know many things about you that simply can't be conveyed through any other medium. The customer will get to know your smile, the tempo of your voice, your sense of humor... they'll even be able to look into your eyes to see if you're being sincere.

The effect is so powerful that you'll be amazed the first time a prospect calls your office and talks to you as if they know you. They've had the equivalent of six "touches" on the internet without your knowledge. All they need now is to talk to you once so that you can answer a few questions and then, they become your customer.

Video Has a High Perceived Value

Video increases your stature. Average people perceive video as "out of reach," so when customers see you in one (even if it's a low-quality internet video) they often get the impression that you must be important.

My business partner and I started video blogging several years ago, and prospects began approaching us at conferences and mixers saying, "You're those guys on the internet!" We had created a bit of local celebrity just by posting a few videos online.

When you start posting videos online, you will be light-years ahead of your competition because most people do not have either the know-how or the willingness to show their face on camera.

Quality vs. Quantity

Many people never get started producing video for their business because they feel like they cannot compete with the production quality that they see on TV, in the movies, or even on the websites of major companies.

It's important to realize that the quality of your online video is much less important than the quantity. Remember that one of the most important functions of video is to let your prospects become familiar with your personality. This can easily be accomplished with a mobile or web camera, posting raw footage to the internet without any edits.

It's tempting to want all the bells and whistles of a great picture, fancy edits, & graphics; but you might find that you want these things for the wrong reasons. The most important thing is to start producing some video, no matter the quality.

When Quality Counts

There is a time and place for quality, but not at the expense of discouraging you from producing video at all. The most important point is that you'd be better off with some low quality video than no video at all.

If you have the budget or the skill to produce some polished video, it's important to know when to spend the time and money on quality and when it's a waste.

Higher-quality video typically works best in more formal settings such as a presentation in a board room, an orientation DVD, or a business overview video on your website.

When Quantity Counts

High quality tends to be wasted in less formal settings such as your blog or email communications. In this case, you main emphasis should be getting some "face" time with your prospects and communicating valuable content.

Ironically, these lower-quality videos (often shot on flip-cams or mobile phones) tend to be more powerful over the long run because they serve the purpose of "warming" your prospects.

When you are planning your online video strategy, divide your content into two categories:

1. Higher quality, more formal video that will be "fixed" in one place on your website or boardroom.
2. Lower quality, less formal video that will be consistently broadcast to your list over time.

Video Blog

The video blog is the simplest, yet one of the most effective video styles available to the online marketer. Simply point a camera at yourself and talk about something for 3–5 minutes. Post the raw video to your blog, YouTube, Facebook, or other social media outlet.

The idea is to deliver a small amount of valuable content to your viewers. Offer free tips, stories, and tidbits to keep them coming back for more. Don't sell too much on these videos; you'll have a chance later when they have become familiar with you.

Try to keep video blogs between 3–5 minutes because attention spans drop sharply after the 3-minute mark.

Here are a few ideas for video blogs:

Whiteboard

Set up your camera on a tripod in front of a whiteboard. Use it to visually describe a concept. The visual representation gives the viewer an alternative mode of understanding your idea and keeps them interested.

Driving

Have a passenger film you on your flip-cam as you drive on your way to a business call. Discuss what you are doing and why.

On Site

Take your mobile camera with you on a customer call. Briefly show how you are adding value by solving a problem.

"Talking Head"

The easiest form of video blogging is to just stand in front of a camera and start talking. Pick an interesting background or simply a solid color.

If your video editing software has the ability to remove a green screen, buy a large green sheet at the fabric store to hang on your wall. The fabric should be stretchy and bright florescent green in color.

What to Do In Front of the Camera

I've been a producer and director for many years and have worked with both professional actors and amateurs. Performing in front of a camera is simple, but can be tricky for some.

In my experience, I've found that there's a phenomenon that happens when a camera is rolling and pointed at a person. While he or she might have been completely relaxed and carrying on casual conversation a minute before; when the camera starts rolling everything seems to change: nerves take over, eyes get glossy, panic takes hold, lines are forgotten, and the mind goes blank.

You might laugh until it happens to you. No one except the most highly skilled actors and actresses are immune from this phenomenon. The trick is to learn to manage it.

There really is no reason to panic, but the mind plays funny tricks on us. When you realize that there is nothing to worry about, you can learn to forget that the camera is even there and just be yourself.

Here are a few tips on what to do when the camera is rolling and pointed at you:

Take a few minutes to warm up

In my experience, it takes the average person about 5–20 minutes to "warm up" in front of a camera. Often times, the best takes are towards the end of the shoot because the subject has loosened up and started to relax.

If you recognize this, you remove the pressure of getting it right on the first take. Tell yourself you are going to do as many takes as you need to get it right.

Ironically, because you've lowered the pressure on yourself, you might just nail the first one.

Make sure the camera is rolling, even during practice

Over the years, I've missed a lot of great takes because my

camera wasn't rolling when the subject was practicing what they were going to say.

People tend to be more natural during practice. The words flow from the heart instead of a script. This is the ideal state to capture on film, and after the moment has passed it can be almost impossible to replicate.

Pretend you're having a conversation with a friend

I always tell my subjects to forget the camera is there and just have a casual conversation with me. If you're shooting yourself, pretend the camera is a close friend and just talk.

A person who watches the video will feel like you are talking to them personally instead of a crowd. This one on one feeling is important when establishing a relationship with a prospect.

Don't act

It happens every time: the first time someone steps in front of the camera, it's like a whole new person takes over their body.

Put away the newscaster voice and the cheesy TV commercial personality inside of you. Just be yourself.

If you catch yourself starting to act, slow down and imagine that you're having a conversation with a single person in your audience. People can sense acting from a mile away.

Don't sweat about being perfect!

In my experience, most people are too caught up trying to be perfect on camera. The fact is: being too polished can work against you.

People want to relate to you, flaws and all. Mistakes prove you are human. It also shows you are confident enough to make mistakes and "roll with the punches."

Getting Started

The most important thing is to just get started. Anyone can afford a $100 flip camera. That's enough to get your videos seen on the internet.

Remember, just be yourself! People want to get to know you, not an actor. Just start putting out video and you'll be amazed how people react to you when they finally meet you in person.

I'll see you on the web!

ABOUT BRIAN

 Brian Lee is a video producer and internet marketing specialist based in Austin, TX. He works with local and national businesses to increase their web footprint with professional quality HD video and leading edge internet marketing strategies. Brian learned his craft in Hollywood where his resume includes work for major television networks, independent films, commercials, and reality television shows. Today, he specializes in reality-style web-based reality shows, video blogs, video sales letters, and commercials.

Learn more at BrianLeeVideo.com.

CHAPTER 17
SOCIAL ACCOUNTS

By Carlos Rosario

Have you heard of any popular social media coupon sites like Groupon or Living Social? Maybe you have tried using one of these types of services in the past?

They are absolutely great at getting many types of businesses a quick influx of money by offering limited quantity, limited time offers that must be redeemed within a certain time frame.

The allure offered by these types of services is the quick amount of cash that a business can generate in such a short amount of time. Some businesses have had far more business than they could handle by offering these types of social coupon offers.

The often unexplored downside of these offers are that many businesses don't fully comprehend the high level implications involved in actually honoring and satisfying the offer requirements, and the possible consequential trade-offs that are undertaken when involved in such obligations.

See, most of the social coupons sites invest heavily building the list of local client subscribers that might be interested in being notified of local bargain deals offered by local businesses in their community willing to offer deep discounts for their otherwise normally priced products and services.

These discounts usually foster the incentives needed to convert new customers from being bystanders to actual patrons of the businesses offering the deal. Most of the people that actually buy the limited offer deals may not have, otherwise, taken part in the offering had the deal not been offered.

The social coupon platform site that facilitates these sales also collect a huge percentage of the sales made for these local company offers, which greatly reduce the profit earned by the local company offering these limited deals.

A typical example might involve a local auto detailing company that offers their normally priced $160 detailing package at a 50% discount on one of these social coupon sites. The coupon offered entitles the coupon voucher buyer to the same level of service that a person paying full price could expect, however the often overlooked caveat is that the social coupon site that made the offer so readily available to the masses gets nearly half of the sales made by that offer.

In the end, this can be a bit hard to swallow. Yes, it is true that without the social coupon site the company making their service available may not have been able to get the word out as efficiently and effectively as the social coupon site with their subscriber list, however taking the little bit of time necessary to build one's own list could have garnered a better return on investment.

What I am suggesting a local business do starting today in order to replicate the types of quick short term returns promised by the social coupon sites is they should start working on building their own lists of prospects to make their limited time offers to.

Here are a few recommendations that a local small business could implement in order to get their own eager list of local clients to market to whenever the occasion warranted.

Easy Ways to Build Your Own List

Ever see those "Place your business card here to win a free lunch (or service or whatever)" style fish bowls at local business point of sale locations?

Who do you think benefits more: the business that is collecting the data base of patrons or the one lucky winner of the sought after prize?

See the smart local business that takes just a little bit of time to harvest these databases is actually taking the time to grow their own diamond fields. They can build a list of local buyers that have actually been in the store and have expressed interest in doing business with the local vendor, if they haven't already actually done so, so these are pre-qualified prospects.

Once the list is compiled and grown, there are limitless ways to market your goods and services to this highly qualified list of prospects that were interested in what you had to offer to begin with.

You can market to your list whenever you like for whatever reason you like and can almost always expect a return on investment whenever you decide to do so.

Here's how this might possibly work:

Let's say that you own a local restaurant and you normally offer faire that is around $14.00 on average. You might be able to collect a list of business cards from patrons by placing a bowl next to your cash register that would allow for patrons to place their cards in there with the notion and incentive that they should expect discounts in their email in box up to 50% (or even free) if the patron includes a legitimate email with their card.

It's only foreseeable that the normal patron would oblige by submitting their details for the hopes of receiving near future offers that would net them huge savings for goods and services that they would have normally paid much more for.

You could send out to this list as often as you like. You could send out your very own time sensitive, limited offers as often as you like. The time limitation generally acts as the sales catalyst because as most people know, people hate not having access to an exclusive something or other.

No one wants to be left out in the cold. Everyone wants to have the deal of a lifetime and even more so to be made to feel smarter for having taken part. Try this method out and see if it's not something that you can't easily indoctrinate and incorporate into your business.

Better yet, to make this even quicker, better, faster and harder why not simply use one of these social coupon sites to net you access to this list of prospects and simply require the prospects that buy the deals to submit their email and other pertinent follow up details to you upon redemption of their pre-paid deals.

You could have a throng of business and a huge influx of money upon demand. You'll definitely never be at a loss for revenue if whatever you are offering is sustainable and sought after.

Try this technique out and give me your feedback to let me know how it worked for you.

Carlos Rosario
Owner of Focused Life Marketing

ABOUT CARLOS

Carlos Rosario is the owner of Focused Life Marketing (insert mission). Originally from Brooklyn, NY he got a degree in Entrepreneurial Studies from Hawaii Pacific University (yes, in Hawaii).

He moved to the San Francisco Bay Area in order to be near his son and now resides in the Silicon Valley, where he runs his home based business. His passion is marketing and he loves to help small business owners figure out creative campaign strategies that will allow them to gain more local market visibility, easily. He's easy to approach and easy to talk to. If you have a marketing question bring it to his attention and be ready to start jotting down notes.

He might chew your ear off but never holds his information back from an eager listener. If you've been looking for local marketing answers then you've found someone ready and willing to give it.

www.FocusedLifeSEM.com

CHAPTER 18
WHY YOUR BUSINESS NEEDS A MOBILE WEBSITE

By Eloise Edwards-Giron

Introduction

Over the years things have changed, including the means by which individuals obtain information, news and other updates. In this age and time everything can be found online. The Internet has become the primary source of information for many people.

With this popularity, marketing on the Internet has become one of the most powerful methods for local businesses to attract more customers.

As technology and the way we communicate evolves, the way we use these channels needs to evolve as well.
One of the next major marketing opportunities is upon us due to the rapid innovations in mobile phones.

In the 70's, when cordless phones were the new thing, it was "mind blowing" to most people, just to have it function without being attached to any wires.

My first memory of hearing about a mobile device was in a science class: the professor was just informing us about the advancement in technology, and that it was predicted that by the year 2000, there would be two major technological innovations.

He said that there would be 1-"Flying Cars" and 2-Smaller Phones" which would be so small, they would be able to fit in our pockets. Both were inconceivable to me at the time! Well, here are we today? Not quite there with the flying cars yet.

But mobile phones are here and in a big way.

Now, why is all this important to Businesses? Because businesses need to be seen where there prospective customers are looking.

And where they are looking is on their mobile devices.
As a Business Owner you should always be on top of what's going on in your industry, know the new trends of business

and how can you implement them into whatever you are doing.

Think about how important having a website has been in a business's ability to market to computer users over the last 10 years. It is now just as important to have a web presence that allows your business to communicate with mobile devices in the form of a Mobile Web Site.

Gartner predicts mobile ad revenue will be US$3.3 billion in 2011. This is estimated to climb to $20.6 billion in 2015 and will continue to grow thereafter.

So what's the difference between a Mobile Website and a regular website?

Regular websites are not optimized for mobile devices. If you've ever tried to view a non-optimized website on a mobile phone you may have noticed how difficult it can be to navigate or find the information you are looking for.

Think about the local customers that are looking for information about your business on their phones. They want to find that information fast and easily.

You want your phone number to be at the top, easy to read and preferably coded so that a mobile phone user can just touch it with their finger to trigger a call.

You also need to have your location and hours of operation prominently posted on the home page for those consumers that are mobile and ready to do business.

Mobile websites are affordable and don't have to replace your current website. In fact a simple modification will allow visitors that arrive at your regular website on their mobile device to automatically be redirected to your mobile website.

I would encourage you not to wait too long before adopting a mobile marketing strategy. Don't think that a smaller version of your regular website will do.

The best way to make the right choice is to think about the way you use your mobile device when looking for local business information. Take note of your browsing habits so you can incorporate the good and avoid the frustrations that can stand in the way of you and potential customers.

ABOUT ELOISE

Eloise Edwards Giron has always being drawn to entrepreneurship, and believes that one must strive to reach their dream in life, as everybody was born with great potential to do so.

Eloise administrated her family local business at an early age in her home town of Limon.

Eloise attended the University of Costa Rica where she obtained a Baccalaureate Degree in Science of Nursing. She later immigrated to the United States where she practices her nursing career in a city hospital in New York.

In her quest of achieving her goal of entrepreneurship, she embarked on a number of businesses and has been developing her skills in with the latest cutting edge principles in Local Internet Marketing.

To learn more about Eloise please visit her site at: http://eloiseedwards-giron.com